CAMBRIDGE Professional English

for work and life
English 365

Personal Study Book 3

with Audio CD

Bob Dignen Steve Flinders Simon Sweeney

CAMBRIDGE
UNIVERSITY PRESS

CAMBRIDGE UNIVERSITY PRESS
Cambridge, New York, Melbourne, Madrid, Cape Town, Singapore,
São Paulo, Delhi

Cambridge University Press
The Edinburgh Building, Cambridge CB2 8RU, UK

www.cambridge.org
Information on this title: www.cambridge.org/9780521549189

First published 2005
5th printing 2009

Printed in Dubai by Oriental Press

A catalogue record for this publication is available from the British Library

ISBN 978-0-521-54918-9 Personal Study Book 3
ISBN 978-0-521-54916-5 Student's Book 3
ISBN 978-0-521-54917-2 Teacher's Book 3
ISBN 978-0-521-54919-6 Student's Book 3 CD (audio) Set
ISBN 978-0-521-54920-2 Student's Book 3 Cassette Set

Contents

Personal Study Book

Introduction 5
Better language learning 6
Better language learning notes 8
Learning diaries 12
Language for language learning 14
Practice exercises 19
Answer key to Practice exercises 49

Personal Study Book Audio CD

Contents of the Audio CD 62

Tapescript
Introduction 63
Part 1 Listening units 64
Part 2 Pronunciation 76

Tapescript: Part 1 Models 80
Answer key to Listening units 84
Learning diaries 88
Track numbers 94
Thanks and acknowledgements 96

English365

Personal Study Book 3

Introduction

Welcome to the *English365* Personal Study Book 3. This book and Audio CD are to help you to practise and learn the English you need for work and for your free time. There are two parts to the book:

Personal Study Book

This **Introduction** tells you about the organisation of the book and CD.

Better language learning gives you ideas about what good learners do to learn more English.

Language for language learning gives you words you must understand for your work in the classroom and for homework.

The **Practice exercises** give you one page of self-study exercises for each unit (1–30) in the *English365* Student's Book 3. You can do one page of exercises after each classroom lesson:
- exercises for type 1 units (Units 1, 4, 7, 10, 13, 16, 19, 22, 25 and 28) practise grammar
- exercises for type 2 units (Units 2, 5, 8, 11, 14, 17, 20, 23, 26 and 29) practise vocabulary and skills you need for your work
- exercises for type 3 units (Units 3, 6, 9, 12, 15, 18, 21, 24, 27 and 30) practise the social skills phrases you need for your work and for your personal life, and general vocabulary.

The **Learning diaries** are to help you keep a record of your own learning experiences and progress.

Personal Study Book Audio CD

The **Listening exercises** are to give you practice in some important areas of social and professional communication. You can listen to the exercises on the CD, write your answers in the book and then check your answers in the Answer key.

The Audio CD also contains **pronunciation** work from the *English365* Student's Book 3 (type 1 units) which you can practise on your own.

The Tapescript for these is at the back of this book. See page 62 for the contents of the CD.

Better language learning

This book and the Audio CD are to help you work between lessons and to remember the work you do with your teacher. You can also help yourself to improve your English using the following ten-point action plan to improve your own learning style.

1 Think about **why** you want to learn.
2 Think about **how important** it is to learn English. If it is important for you and your job, you will give it a lot of time. But remember: it is difficult to learn a language well without classroom lessons <u>and</u> practice outside the classroom.
3 Decide **how much time** you can give to your English. You can learn a lot in five or ten minutes per day. Little and often is best.
4 Think about **what** you want to learn. Plan achievable objectives for each day, each week and each month.
5 Think about **how** you learn. For example, do you like to hear new language or to write it down or to see it on the page? What personal approaches work best for you?
6 **Plan** your work and set targets for the day, the week and the month to come.
7 **Reward** yourself. Give yourself a present when you reach a goal.
8 **Think about** yourself **learning and speaking** English **well**. Adopt a positive attitude. This 'mental modelling' is good for your learning.
9 Keep **a diary** (see pages 12 and 88). Good learners think about their learning. Write about:
   • what you study
   • when you study
   • how you feel about your study.
10 **Review** your work. We often don't learn something the first time we do it. Instead, we often have to do something three or more times before we can do it well.

Use pages 8–11 to write your own learning plan. You may also discuss some of these questions with your teacher and with other people in your class. Thinking about the questions before you talk about them also helps your learning.

PLAN
what you are going to learn.
Have clear goals.

PRACTISE
what you are learning.

REVIEW
what you have learnt.

For more ideas about improving the way you learn, look at *Learning to Learn English* by Gail Ellis and Barbara Sinclair, published by Cambridge University Press.

Better language learning notes

Write your own notes to help you improve your English more efficiently. It's a good idea to write your answers in pencil, since your answers to some questions may change as your English improves.

It's not necessary to answer all the questions, but answering some of them – even just one or two – will help you think about your learning and help you to be a better learner. Choose the questions you think are the most useful and work on them.

Step 1: Why do I want to learn English?

1 ....

2 ....

3 ....

Notes:

Step 2: How important is it for me to learn English?

Learning English is:
Very important
Quite important
Not very important
Not at all important

Notes:

Step 3: How much time can I give to my English?

I can give:

5 minutes a day ▩
10 minutes a day ▩
15 minutes a day ▩
20 minutes a day ▩
30 minutes a day ▩
45 minutes a day ▩
60 minutes a day ▩

Notes:

Step 4: What do I want to learn?

Write in pencil and use an eraser so that you can change your objectives each day/week/month.

My objectives for today are:

1 ....

2 ....

3 ....

My objectives for this week are:

1 ....

2 ....

3 ....

My objectives for this month are:

1 ....

2 ....

3 ....

Notes:

Step 5: How do I learn?

When I am learning English I like to ....

When I am learning English I don't much like to ....

Some approaches and methods that seem to work for me include ....

....

Notes:

Step 6: What is my plan for my learning?

Today I plan to do these activities: ....

This week I plan to do these activities: ....

This month I plan do these activities: ....

Notes:

Step 7: How will I reward myself if I do everything in my plan?

My reward for this week's work will be ....

My reward for this month's work will be ....

A long-term reward will be ....

Notes:

Step 8: What are the really positive things about my use of English?

Think about yourself using English. Write down:

- What do I do well?...
- An example of a recent improvement: ....
- My major achievements in English: ....
- What can I do to consolidate and build on these achievements? ....
  ....

Notes:

Step 9: How do I keep a diary of my learning? (See pages 12–13 and 88–93.)

Use this checklist:

• Which diary (or diaries) will I use? ....
• Will I write in it (them) every day/week/month? ....

Notes:

Step 10: Is revision part of my language learning?

Do I review my work? ....
What should I review? ....
How often should I review? ....
Can I be more systematic in revising my English? ....

Notes:

Final question. Ask yourself from time to time:

• Am I making progress?
• Am I achieving my objectives?
• What is stopping me from achieving my objectives?

Notes:

Learning diaries

Introduction
This Personal Study Book contains six learning diaries (pages 88–93) to help you keep a record of your own learning experiences and progress (Grammar, Communication skills, Vocabulary, Speaking fluently, Pronunciation, Understanding).

How to use these diaries
Use these diaries to note down six key points about your learning.

1 Progress   Which areas of your English you have improved.
2 Classroom learning   Which classroom activities helped you improve.
3 Self-study   What you have done outside the classroom to practise or develop your language.
4 Problems   What you find most difficult to improve and why.
5 Priorities   Which area is the most important for you to focus on in grammar, communication skills, vocabulary, speaking fluently, pronunciation or understanding.
6 Action plan   How you can improve your English in the future.

Why use learning diaries
By using learning diaries you can:
- stay motivated by noting down areas where you have improved
- speed up your learning by identifying the right learning methods for you
- use English more accurately by focusing on typical mistakes or problems
- motivate yourself to spend time learning English outside the classroom
- maximise your efforts by identifying your key learning objectives
- ensure you reach learning objectives by defining personal action plans

How many diaries to use
You should decide how many learning diaries you want to use. Select a diary (or diaries) which will help you improve an area of your language skills which you think is important for you. If you want to concentrate on grammar, just keep the grammar diary. If you want to focus on speaking, you could keep diaries for communication skills and speaking fluently. Some people will use all six diaries. Select which you think is best for you. It would be a good idea to discuss your selection briefly with your teacher.

How often to use learning diaries
You should decide how often to use your learning diaries – after each lesson, after every three units, once a month, etc. If you decide to use your diaries very often, it is a good idea before you start to make photocopies of the blank learning diary pages in your Personal Study Book, write your notes on the photocopies and then keep these completed pages in a special folder for future reference. Alternatively, type out the diary pages and keep an electronic copy in your computer. The most important thing is to use your diaries regularly.

What to write
Everyone has a different style when it comes to keeping diaries (see example opposite). Start by writing down what is important to you, but compare what

you have written with your colleagues in class. Remember, the main objective is to support your learning, so write down thoughts, experiences and tips for yourself which will help you learn faster in the future.

How often to review

Review your experiences of learning by reading through your diaries regularly so you can identify ways to make your English learning as effective as possible.

Diary extracts

This extract will give you some ideas about what you can write in your own learning diary.

Learning diary 1: Grammar

Progress	Which areas of my grammar have improved? My tenses are much better but I'm still not sure when to use present simple and present continuous.
Classroom learning	Which learning activities in the classroom helped me learn grammar? Actually speaking the grammar in role-plays helped me to remember. Writing the grammar exercises is easy but it doesn't help me learn.
Self-study	What have I done outside the classroom to practise or improve my grammar? Haven't done much recently.
Problems	Which grammar mistakes do I still find it difficult to correct? I keep making mistakes with 'since'.
Priorities	Which grammar areas should I focus on now? I think I need to improve my control of the tenses, especially when asking questions.

Future learning action plan
Every time you write in your grammar diary, note down any other experiences, thoughts or feelings about developing your grammar, particularly any *new ideas* you have for learning, which can help you create an action plan to improve more quickly in the future.
I will write some example sentences with 'since' on pieces of paper and stick them to my computer to help me remember.
Worry less about grammar! It's more important for me at the moment to be more fluent.

Language for language learning
Guide to grammar terms

These are words we use to talk about English grammar. You may already have met some of these terms in Books 1 and 2, and we have added more for Book 3. They will help you understand the grammar work you do in the classroom and for homework. Use your dictionary to write your own translation of words you don't know.

Active (adjective/noun)
An active verb or sentence is one in which the subject does the action. For example, 'She gave him a present.' See **Passive**.

Auxiliary verb (noun phrase)
A verb which is used with another verb to form tenses, negatives and questions: 'be', 'have' and 'do' are the three auxiliary verbs in English.

Chunking (noun)
The separation of speech into parts (chunks) divided by clear pauses. Each chunk usually conveys a specific meaning. Even quite rapid speech often contains examples of chunking.

Collocation (noun)
A word or phrase that is frequently used with another word or phrase in a way that sounds correct. Examples of two-word collocations: 'target audience', 'mass marketing', 'public relations'.

Comparative (adjective)
The form of an adjective or adverb that is used to show that someone or something has more of something than someone or something else. For example, 'better' is the comparative form of 'good' and 'smaller' is the comparative form of 'small'. See **Superlative**.

Compound noun (noun phrase)
A noun made up of two nouns together. For example, 'travel insurance', 'computer virus'.

Conditional (adjective)
A conditional sentence often contains 'if' or 'unless'. One half of the sentence expresses something which is dependent on the other half.

Connecting words or phrases (noun phrase)
Words that link ideas in speech or writing. There are many connecting words in English including conjunctions: 'and', 'but'; listing words: 'first', 'second', 'then', 'finally'; words that refer to consequences: 'so', 'therefore'; and result: 'as a result', 'because of'.

Consonant (noun)
A letter of the alphabet that is not a vowel: 'b' and 'c' are consonants, 'a' and 'e' are not consonants. See **Vowel**.

Countable (adjective/noun)
A noun with a singular and plural form. For example, 'girl' and 'girls'. See **Uncountable**.

Direct speech (noun phrase)
The exact words that someone says. For example, in 'He shouted, "Go away"!', 'Go away' is direct speech. See **Reported speech**.

Emphatic stress (noun phrase)
Stress emphasises something to show that it is important. Emphatic stress is used to make meaning clearer, especially to emphasise a speaker's opinion or to correct a misunderstanding. For example, 'I said I **didn't** phone the doctor. I asked **you** to do it!'

Future reference (noun phrase)
The different ways you can refer to events in the future. The present tense, the present continuous tense, 'will', the future continuous tense and 'going to' can all be used to talk about the future.

Infinitive (noun)
The root form of a verb preceded by the particle 'to'. For example, 'to speak', 'to work'.

Minimal pair (noun phrase)
Two words that differ in only one sound. For example, 'sheep' and 'ship', 'price' and 'prize'.

Modal verb (noun phrase)
A verb which is used before another verb to show that something is possible, necessary, etc. For example, 'can', 'must', 'may', etc.

Multi-word verb (noun phrase)
A verb that has more than one word in it. For example, 'talk about', 'work out', 'look forward to'.

Particle (noun)
A word which has a grammatical purpose but often little meaning. For example, in 'I tidied up the room', 'up' is a particle.

Passive (adjective/noun)
A passive verb or sentence is one in which the subject does not do or perform the action but is affected by it. For example, 'He was given the top job' is a passive sentence. See **Active**.

Pause(s) (noun)
A break or short silence in speech. Pauses are an important part of speech and can highlight meaning. For example, 'He told me that Maria was (*pause*) not coming' suggests interesting, good, bad or surprising news.

Phoneme (noun)
The smallest contrastive unit in the sound system of a language. For example, /p/ and /b/. See the pronunciation symbols on page 115 in the Student's Book.

Pronoun (noun)
A word that is used instead of a noun which has usually already been talked about. For example, 'she', 'it', 'mine', etc.

Quantifier (noun)
A word or group of words which is used before a noun to show an amount of that noun. For example, 'much', 'many' and 'a lot' are quantifiers.

Reported speech (noun phrase)
Reported speech (also called indirect speech) 'reports' what someone said. For example, 'Come quickly' can be reported as 'She told me to come quickly.' See **Direct speech**.

Reporting verb (noun phrase)
A verb that is commonly used (in the past tense) in reported speech. Examples of reporting verbs are 'say', 'tell', 'report', 'state', 'advise'.

Rule (noun)
A rule tells us something about how a system, for example, a grammar system works. For example, the rule about making questions with the verb 'to be' in English tells us to change the order of the subject and the verb: 'He is happy' → 'Is he happy?'

Schwa (noun)
The schwa is the pronunciation symbol /ə/ as in 'teacher' → /tiːtʃə/ and 'opposite' → /ɒpəzɪt/.

Silent (adjective)
A silent letter in a word is one which you do not pronounce. For example, the 'b' in 'doubt'.

Stress (verb/noun)
To pronounce a word or syllable with greater force than other words in the same sentence or another syllable in the same word.

Stress pattern (noun phrase)
A rule which tells you where the stress will fall. For example, for words ending in '-ation', the stress always falls on the next-to-last syllable.

Superlative (noun)
The form of an adjective or adverb that is used to show that someone or something has more of something than anyone or anything else. For example, 'best' is the superlative of 'good'. See **Comparative**.

Syllable (noun)
A word or part of a word that has one vowel sound. For example, 'important' has three syllables.

Uncountable (adjective/noun)
A noun which does not have a plural form and cannot be used with 'a' or 'one'. For example, 'music' and 'furniture' are uncountable nouns. See **Countable**.

Vowel (noun)
A speech sound that you make with your lips and teeth open. The five vowels in English are 'a', 'e', 'i', 'o' and 'u'. See **Consonant**.

Other language for language learning

These are other words that you will meet in *English365* Book 3 and which you will need to understand to do exercises and classroom activities. Use your dictionary to write your own translation of words you don't know.

Active listening (noun phrase)
The things you say and the signals you give when listening to someone to show your understanding and interest. For example, words and phrases like 'Yes', 'OK', 'I understand'; sounds like 'Aha', 'mmm'; and signals like nodding the head and maintaining eye contact.

Argue (verb)
To give reasons to support or oppose an idea.

Bargain (verb)
The process of reaching an agreement between two or more people in which each promises to do something in exchange for something else. See **Negotiate**.

Benefits (noun)
The advantages you get from doing certain things or making particular choices.

Down-toning (noun) Down-tone (verb)
Being less formal, less direct or less critical in speech or written communication. For example, 'This work is hopeless' → 'This work is not very satisfactory.'

Explain (verb)
To make something clear or easy to understand by giving reasons for it or details about it.

Extract (noun)
A particular part of a book, poem, etc.

Fact (noun)
Something which is known to have happened or to exist, especially something for which proof exists. For example, 'London is the capital of the United Kingdom.' See **Opinion**.

Flowchart (noun)
A diagram – often with boxes joined by arrows to show direction – which shows the stages of a process.

Formal (adjective)
Language, clothes and behaviour that are serious and correct. See **Informal**.

Headline (noun)
A line of words in large letters as the title of a story in a newspaper.

Informal (adjective)
Language, clothes and behaviour that are suitable when you are with friends or family, but not for official occasions. See **Formal**.

Link (verb)
To make a connection between two or more things.

Match (verb)
If two things match, they go together well in terms of type, meaning or appearance.

Mind map (noun phrase)
A diagram with lines and circles for organising information so that it is easier to use or remember.

Model (verb/noun)
Someone who or something which is an example for others to copy.

Motivate (verb)
To make someone want to do something.

Negotiate (verb)
To discuss with another person or group of people and reach an agreement which is acceptable to both sides, for example over prices, actions or contracts. See **Bargain**.

Opinion (noun)
A thought or belief about something or someone. See **Fact**.

Perform (verb)
To carry out or do something, especially in front of other people.

Persuade (noun)
To get someone to do something that you want him/her to do. For example, 'I persuaded her to come with me.'

Phrase (noun)
A group of words which is part rather than the whole of a sentence.

Predict (verb)
To say what you think will happen in the future.
Prepare (verb)
To get ready for something.
Proactive (adjective)
Doing something to cause change rather than waiting for change to happen.
Procedure (noun)
The usual way of doing something.
Progress report (noun phrase)
A document or presentation which is usually formal and describes what has happened up to now in a project.
Rapport (noun)
A good understanding of someone and an ability to communicate well with them.
Recommend (verb)
To say that someone or something is good or suitable for a particular purpose.
Register (noun)
The style of speech or writing that indicates formality or informality. For example, compare 'Can you lend me a fiver?' (informal British English) with 'I would like to request a loan from the bank' (formal).
Role (noun)
Actors play roles in films. Students play the roles of different people in role-play exercises in the language classroom.
Sequence (noun)
A series of related things which have a particular order.
Skill (noun)
An ability to do an activity or job well, especially because you have practised it. See **Social skills**.
Small talk (noun phrase)
Conversation about unimportant things, often between people who do not know each other well.
Social skills (noun phrase)
The ability to communicate successfully with other people, especially in informal and non-work related situations. See **Skill**.
Unscramble (verb)
To discover the meaning of information given in a secret or complicated way. For example, if a group of words have been mixed up, you unscramble them when you put them into the right order.
Visual support (noun phrase)
Anything used by a speaker in a presentation or meeting to illustrate what he/she is saying. For example, a graph, drawing, picture, chart, diagram or table.
Word family (noun phrase)
A group of words with the same stem and a shared meaning, which are different parts of speech (verb, noun, adjective, etc.). For example, 'industrialise', 'industry', 'industrial'.

Practice exercises

Grammar: Present simple and continuous; present perfect simple and continuous – Introducing an organisation

1 Complete the information about a company in the Caribbean with the correct form of the verb. Sometimes more than one answer is possible.

What does Caribcruise do? Caribcruise is a small company which
(1) .... (organise) sailing holidays in the Caribbean from its base on Martinique. The company (2) .... (provide) the experience of a lifetime for its customers for the last ten years. It now (3) .... (own) 20 yachts and (4) .... (receive) several awards for the quality of its service.
What's new? At the moment we (5) .... (expand) our operations. What's more, our new online booking system (6) .... (let) you check availability to destinations 24 hours a day. Still need convincing? You can look at our picture gallery which we (7) .... (develop) recently. It will inspire you to join us.

Grammar: Present simple and continuous; present perfect simple and continuous – Keeping small talk going

2 Two people meet on holiday. Complete the conversation with the correct form of the verb.
A: So, where (1) .... ? (you / stay)
B: At the Palm Strip Hotel. In fact, we always stay there.
A: Really? How long (2) .... to Guadeloupe? (you / come)
B: For over ten years! So how long (3) .... here? (you / be)
A: Since Friday.
B: And how often (4) .... to this part of the world? (you / come)
A: We (5) .... to the Caribbean before. (never / be)
B: I'm lucky – I (6) .... (run) a small company on Martinique.
A: Sounds good. What (7) .... exactly? (you / do)
B: It's a sailing holiday company.
A: That must be fun.

Over to you

Imagine meeting the owner of Caribcruise. Write some polite small talk questions he/she could ask you using these tenses. Then write down your answers to the questions.

Unit 2

Work vocabulary: Managing organisations

1 Complete the management qualities checklist with words from the box.

1 The best managers should be able to accept ....

2 Management involves providing good ....

3 Managers should lead ....

4 Staff need the freedom to be ....

5 Anyone can make ....

6 Everyone in an organisation needs to learn
from ....

7 All organisations need to develop effective
communication ....

8 Everyone needs to work together to .... problems.

> sort out
> by example
> channels
> mistakes
> responsibility
> experience
> leadership
> creative

Professional communication: Writing 1 – Emails and register

2 Sort out two emails. One is to a work colleague and the other is to a new professional contact from another organisation. In each line there is a third alternative which does not fit in either email.

1 a Hi Alex, b Dear Mr Nicoletti, c Hello,

2 a Why didn't you go? b I was pleased to get your message. c You really shouldn't be working.

3 a I thought you were having the day off. b It would be good if we can meet when you come to London. c I only read my emails once a month.

4 a Please let me know the exact dates of your visit. b Why don't you forget all about work when you're not here? c I've got a boring meeting later today.

5 a Sorry, I can't help, I don't know what Jack decided. b I'm planning a report on Tasmania. c Will your colleague Ms Costanza be with you?

6 a The conference will start with a big dinner. b Perhaps we can organise a half-day meeting. c You could ring him on his mobile.

7 a We are organising a trip to Paris. b Or maybe if you want I'll tell him to call you. c Do let me know if I can send you any information to help you before then.

8 a Looking forward to hearing from you. b I'll send you an outline of the project. c See you soon.

9 a (*nothing*) b Yours faithfully, c Best wishes,

10 a *Your first name only* b *Your first name and your family name* c *Your email address*

Over to you

Think of an organisation you know well – perhaps the one you work for. Write a paragraph about the way it is managed.

General communication: Getting started

1 **Change one word in each sentence to improve these attempts to start up a conversation with someone.**
   1 Hello, I don't know someone here.
   2 Do you think if I talk to you?
   3 Excuse me, is anyone lying here?
   4 So you work in the hospital. What do you make there?
   5 I've always wanted to introduce a film producer.
   6 Do you sleep here or are you just a visitor?
   7 I'm on computers.
   8 What do you eat of the food?

2 **Which of the sentences in exercise 1 do these responses (a–d) best follow?**
   a I'm just here for the conference.
   b No, it's free. Go ahead.
   c Really? My brother works in IT.
   d Not at all. I don't know anyone here either.

General vocabulary: Newspaper headlines

3 **The words in the first box are often used in newspaper headlines. Match the words in the first box with words with a similar meaning in the second.**

| talks | envoy | poll | coup | blaze | aid |
| key | go-ahead | jet | halt | head | blast |

| stop | discussions | help | diplomat | explosion | lead | approval | fire |
| important | aeroplane | change of government | | survey of public opinion | | | |

Over to you

Write some sentences you could use to start up a conversation with someone you don't know.

Unit 4

Grammar: Verb grammar – Explaining benefits

1 Complete the WebWatch advertisement by choosing the correct form.

WebWatch – Available Today

1 want   We just want *to take / that we take* three minutes of your time.
2 promise   We promise *not to / that we not* waste your time.
3 tell   We must tell *you / to you* about our latest intelligent WebWatch.
4 let   It lets *that you / you* tell the time anywhere in the world.
5 allow   It also allows *that you / you to* surf the internet at any time.
6 suggest   We suggest you *visit / visiting* one of our shops today.
7 decide   If you decide *to buy / buying* one in January, you can take advantage of our special offer.
8 make   We'll make *to you / you* an offer you can't refuse!

Grammar: Verb grammar – Talking about products

2 Read the WebWatch customer feedback and match each sentence to the correct context.

1 I stopped checking my email on my WebWatch during the meeting. ▓
2 I stopped to check my email on my WebWatch during the meeting. ▓
   a *I wanted to see if I'd received any important emails.*
   b *I couldn't concentrate on what people were saying.*
3 I tried to use my watch to deal with emails when travelling on business. ▓
4 I tried using my watch to deal with emails when travelling on business. ▓
   a *It was a great idea but I couldn't make it work.*
   b *I wanted to do it as an experiment.*
5 I didn't remember to buy a second set of batteries for the watch. ▓
6 I didn't remember buying a second set of batteries for the watch. ▓
   a *Now the current batteries are flat and the watch doesn't work.*
   b *But I obviously did it because I found some in my briefcase.*
7 I like using new gadgets such as this watch. ▓
8 I like to use new gadgets such as this watch. ▓
   a *It's a good way to stay informed about new developments in technology.*
   b *It's fun.*

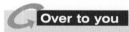
Over to you

Use the verbs on this page to write sentences which you could use in an email or during a meeting or phone call about your products or services.

Work vocabulary: Financial planning and control

1 Replace the words in italics with a verb from the box.

schedule	forecast	compile	prepare a budget	overrun	break even
borrow	lend	invest in	charge	assess	control

Most people need to (1) *get someone to lend them* money at some point in their lives. Banks are always happy to (2) *release money to customers* because they can (3) *ask for* interest and so make a profit. Businesses, like ordinary people, do the same, especially if they need to (4) *spend money on* new projects. Businesses have to (5) *plan the costs and expenditure* for the project and work out when it will (6) *begin to make a profit*. This requires the project team to (7) *plan the key events over* the project and (8) *estimate future* costs and income over a given time period. It is necessary to (9) *work out and present* detailed accounts for the project and (10) *limit* costs, or the project will (11) *cost more than* its budget. Any individual or business that wants to borrow money needs to (12) *make a judgement about* their circumstances and the future financial environment.

Professional communication: Presenting 1 – Progress reports

2 Look at the outline of a short presentation on an urban regeneration project. Match a sentence (a–f) with each part of the talk (1–6).

1 What people already know
2 Current situation
3 Next steps
4 What has been done
5 Action needed now
6 Expected results

a *When we have done that, we will start* looking for financial support from local organisations and companies.
b *The immediate priority now is to* identify all the interested organisations who can help the project go forward.
c *Right now we are carrying out* local research and general planning.
d *As we all know, this project* was created because we understand we have to attract more businesses to the area.
e *We expect that in four years' time there will be* many new businesses moving into the area and we will be reporting a success story.
f *We have already produced* a detailed report on the strengths and weaknesses of the area *and we have identified* what has to be done.

Over to you

Think of some work you have been involved in. Write a progress report about the work using some of the phrases in italics above.

Unit 6

General communication: Building rapport

1 Match the two halves of the sentences to make expressions for building rapport with someone you have just met.

1 What do you do ...   a ... the chance to do that.
2 Really? I'm interested ...   b ... in your spare time?
3 Are you ...   c ... quite fascinating.
4 That sounds ...   d ... a cyclist as well?
5 I'd love to have ...   e ... in astronomy too.

General vocabulary: Current affairs and economic issues

2 Mike Fortune is a politician. He wants people to vote for him. Match his promises (1–8) with the policy areas in the box.

> full employment   privatisation   natural environment   recreation facilities
> waste disposal   traffic congestion   health services   housing

'My party promises to:
1 sell off government-owned companies.
2 clean up the air and dirty rivers.
3 provide safe places for children to play and more swimming pools.
4 train more doctors and nurses and build more hospitals.
5 reduce the number of cars in towns and on motorways.
6 build houses at prices which are affordable for ordinary working people.
7 make sure that everyone who wants a job can get one.
8 have someone collect your household rubbish every week.'

3 Complete these word families. There is more than one word in three cases.

Verb	Person noun	General noun	Adjective
	consumer	(2)	x
		(2)	economic (+1)
x		environment	
			political
		education	

Over to you

Write a paragraph about the big current affairs and economic issues in your country. Which do you think are the most important and why?

Grammar: Past simple, past continuous and past perfect simple – Describing personal history

1 Complete the biography of Bill Gates by choosing the correct verb form.

Born William Henry Gates III in Seattle on October 28th 1955, Bill Gates (1) *came / was coming* from a long line of entrepreneurs and public figures. Early on in life, Bill Gates showed that he (2) *had inherited / inherited* the ambition, intelligence and competitive spirit that (3) *was helping / had helped* the other members of his family rise to the top in their chosen professions. His parents therefore (4) *had decided / decided* to enrol him in Lakeside, a private school. Bill Gates, Paul Allen and a few other Lakeside students immediately (5) *had become / became* inseparable from the school's computer, staying in the computer room all day and night, leading to ongoing problems: they (6) *handed in / were handing in* homework late (if at all) and (7) *skipped / skipping* classes to be in the computer room. In late 1968, Bill Gates, Paul Allen and two other hackers from Lakeside (8) *were forming / formed* the Lakeside Programmers Group in order to break into business. Their first opportunity (9) *had arisen / arose* with Computer Center Corporation hiring the students to find bugs in their computer system. As a result, Gates and Allen really (10) *were beginning / began* to develop the talents that would lead to the formation of Microsoft seven years later.

Grammar: Past simple, past continuous and past perfect simple – Describing past experiences

2 Choose the correct verb form to complete the computer stories.
Installation horror 'I (1) .... (install) some new software when there (2) .... (be) a power cut so I (3) .... (have to) start all over again!'
Laptop crash 'My laptop (4) .... (crash) while I (5) .... (set up) for an important presentation.'
Teenage blues 'Last week I (6) .... (turn on) my laptop at work and (7) .... (discover) my teenage son (8) .... (manage) to delete the entire hard disk when downloading a game.'
Installation luck 'The installation of the software (9) .... (finish) before the power cut so I (10) .... (not / have to) reinstall it.'

 **Over to you**

Write some stories about interesting events in your life using the tenses in this unit.

Unit 8

Work vocabulary: Politics

1 Complete the text with words from the box.

> stakeholders   health authority   global citizenship   trade unions
> strategic partnerships   Chamber of Commerce   city council

International links and global citizenship

Most local authorities understand the need for (1) .... in
promoting business development. These include working with different
(2) .... including local government, industry and educational
institutions. Many organisations join local business associations, such as
a (3) .... , which have international links. These promote
trade, but also a sense of (4) .... in communities. Sometimes
central or local government bodies, for example a (5) .... ,
provide grants to set up new enterprises or build international links.
Large local employers, such as a (6) .... , can help to build a
sense of global responsibility, and of course (7) .... have
always had a sense of international solidarity among workers.

Professional communication: Presenting 2 – Structuring

2 You have to give a talk about your organisation's internet marketing
plans, following the outline on the slide below. Write sentences you
could use for the different parts of the talk (1–7).

> **Internet marketing –**
> **Developing e-prospects**
> 1 General marketing approach –
>   the background
> 2 Current web use –
>   strengths and weaknesses
> 3 New initiatives
> **Questions and discussion**

1 Greet your audience.
2 Explain the title of your talk.
3 Tell them it's in three parts.
4 Explain the structure in a little more detail using the slide shown here.
5 Explain your policy on questions and discussion.
6 Begin the first part of your talk.
7 End the first part and link to the second part.

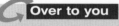 **Over to you**

Prepare the plan of a presentation about your work and write down six key phrases
which you would use in it.

General communication: Listening

1 Here are some examples of what good listeners say. Put the words into the right order in each sentence. Two of them are questions.
   1 interesting really that's
   2 happened me what tell then
   3 did where go you exactly
   4 wonderful that sounds really
   5 mean you see I what
   6 and how feel that about did you
   7 have difficult been must very that
   8 if it as time a you sounds had great

2 Match the verbs (1–5) with the sentences (a–e) to complete each of these ideas for better listening.
   1 Check   a ... that you're listening.
   2 Influence   b ... signals to the other person which say 'I'm
   3 Make   paying attention.'
   4 Show   c ... your understanding of details.
   5 Send   d ... sure you understand.
                      e ... the direction of the conversation by asking
                          follow-up questions.

General vocabulary: The weather

3 Complete the weather forecast with words from the box.

   gale   spells   breezes   rain   forecast   showers   ground   wind   temperatures

   1 There will be some sunny .... in the morning.
   2 In the afternoon, there will be sleet and scattered snow
     .... , especially in the north-east.
   3 The west will be cold with a biting northerly ....
   4 Gentle .... will blow in from the west later on.
   5 This will cause .... to drop a little in the afternoon.
   6 In the south there will be outbreaks of .... later today.
   7 Tomorrow, ... force winds are likely on high ....
   8 The .... for later in the week is good, with plenty of
     sunshine but also the risk of some showers.

Over to you

Write down what the weather is like where you live at the moment. Then write down a typical day's weather in six months' time.

Unit 10

Grammar: Multi-word verbs – Giving opinions about technology

1 Read some opinions about mobile phones (a–h). Decide if the multi-word verbs in italics are Type 1, 2, 3 or 4 verbs. Use a dictionary to help you if necessary.

1 Verb + particle (without an object)
2 Verb + particle + object (verb and particle can be separated)
3 Verb + particle + object (verb and particle cannot be separated)
4 Verb + particle + particle + object (verb and particles cannot be separated)

a I love my mobile. The first thing I do in the morning is *turn it on*.
b I use my phone mostly to *look at* share prices on the internet.
c I use the notepad on my phone to *note down* ideas that I have during the day.
d I hate *waiting about* when people don't text to tell me they're going to be late.
e I'm *building up* a collection of mobile phones. I have over 20 now.
f I'm *looking forward to* next year when the next generation of phones will be launched.
g I think mobile manufacturers are too *focused on* gimmicks. I just use a phone to make calls.
h I hate mobile phones. People should *switch them off* during meetings.

Grammar: Multi-word verbs – Discussing project problems

2 Read these sentences from an email about project problems and replace one verb in each sentence with the multi-word verbs in brackets. If the multi-word verb is separable, write down the two possible answers. Use a dictionary to help you if necessary.

1 We have encountered a few problems during the software installation. (run up against)
2 I'm not sure when we will overcome the problems. (get round)
3 This means postponing installation until next year. (put off)
4 I hope you can accept this. (live with)
5 We will try to recover the time later in the project. (make up)
6 I'll calculate the cost of any delays. (work out)
7 I'm confident we can respect the initial budget. (stick to)
8 If you want to discuss this, please call me. (talk about)

Over to you

Choose eight multi-word verbs (including four not listed in the exercises above) and use them in an email to a friend or colleague asking for help with a problem.

Work vocabulary: Quality

1 Match the phrases (1–6) with the correct definition (a–f).

1 quality control
2 production-oriented
3 customer needs
4 visual checks
5 automated systems
6 satisfaction surveys

a manufacturing that focuses on speed, efficiency and quantity
b quality control that depends on people looking at finished products
c production processes controlled by computers
d research on customer opinion some time after they purchase products
e ways to improve quality of goods or services
f what customers or consumers want

2 Complete these sentences about ways to improve quality.

1 Recruit only p......................... and highly s......................... staff.
2 Introduce in-company t......................... p......................... .
3 Build a......................... s......................... into production processes.
4 Train staff to carry out v......................... c......................... .
5 Always respond to c......................... f......................... .
6 Improve e......................... at all levels in the organisation.

Professional communication: Meetings 1 – Listening and helping understanding

3 Complete the text with words from the box.

| written report or notes | keep eye contact | first, then, next, finally | slowly and clearly |
| There are three points | repeat or summarise | keep to the point | |

In a meeting, try to help people to understand you. Speak (1) ....
at all times. (2) .... key information and check that people
understand. It may sometimes be useful in a meeting or a presentation
to supply a brief (3) .... in a handout. Always organise what
you say, (4) .... and keep things simple. Sequencing language
such as (5) .... is very helpful. It also helps to list things by
saying, for example: (6) '......................... to emphasise: first ..., second ...,
third ...'. When you are talking, (7) .... and think about your
audience.

Over to you

Think of your own organisation. Write a paragraph about how it ensures quality in its products and services.

Unit 12

General communication: Dealing with 'no'

1 Use words from the box to complete sentences you can use when someone says no to you.

> disappointed   minute   find   hoping   help   honest   positive
> through   way   affect   solution   look   afraid

1 Just a .... Can we talk this .... ?
2 I was .... you might say that.
3 To be .... , I was .... for something more ....
4 I have to say that I'm rather ....
5 Is there another .... we can .... at this?
6 I'd like to try and .... another ....
7 Have you thought about how this will .... the project?
8 Would it .... if I worked next weekend instead?

2 Which of the above sentences do these sentences (a–d) best answer?
a No, I'm afraid that will be too late.
b I'm afraid that that's the best we can offer.
c I'm sorry to hear that but it won't change my mind.
d We've already considered all the options.

General vocabulary: TV and TV programmes

3 Match words from the box with these sentences about TV.

> plot   satellite   rating   repeat   recording   channel
> scheduling   individual performance   listings magazine

1 It's on BBC2 at 10.30.
2 I thought Brad Pitt was fantastic.
3 It's about this man who wakes up to discover he's only 10 years old.
4 I think it's on at 9 o'clock. Just wait a minute while I check.
5 They've given it five stars and it's a 12 so everyone can watch it.
6 I put the tape in and I put the timer on but it didn't record.
7 There's football on three different channels. I'd like more choice.
8 I missed it when it first came out. I'm glad they're showing it again.
9 We get all the terrestrial channels and then we have a special aerial that gets lots of extra channels as well.

 Over to you

Write a description of a programme you've seen on TV which was important to you. What was it about and why was it important?

Grammar: Modal verbs to express certainty – Discussing office news

1 Choose the correct form of the verb in italics to complete this email, which relates to the emails on page 47 in the Student's Book.

Hi Jacques,
Back in the office again! Good to hear Mexico went well. I'm sure it (1) *must / may* have been very tough with all that travelling. Getting your report at the end of the week (2) *should / might* be fine so don't panic! Regarding the Arc invoice, Accounts informed me that it (3) *could / can* be a database problem which is why we're not finding a record. They're checking. But we (4) *must / should* have received it because Arc told me they sent it by courier and they have confirmation of delivery.
About the cancelled training, I'm not 100% sure but Louis (5) *might take / might have taken* the decision as four of the team are off work sick. I'm very busy today, but looking at my schedule it seems that I (6) *should / must* have time to call you later to clarify the above points. I'll check and get back to you asap.
Judith

Grammar: Modal verbs to express certainty – Discussing possibilities

2 Two managers are discussing the appointment of a team leader. Complete the dialogue using a modal with the correct form of the verb in brackets.

A: So, it's clear. You think we (1) .... (appoint) Karl as team leader because you know him best and you've coached him so much.

B: Yes and no. He (2) .... (be) under-qualified for this position. It's a possibility.

A: Surely not. He (3) .... (have) the necessary training last year to qualify as a level 2 manager. Or am I wrong?

B: I'm not sure. He (4) .... (be) in Japan when we ran the training. If so, he didn't do it. I'll have to check with him.

A: You know, you (5) .... (be) right. And if he was in Japan, he (6) .... (be) qualified for level 2 management.

B: I know. But let's wait and see. He (7) .... (receive) the invitation to apply two hours ago. It's up to him to make a decision about applying.

A: Yes, and anyway, it (8) .... (be) a big problem. We can always give him the training if we think he should get the job.

Over to you

Your colleague is not in the office and your boss asks you where he/she is. Write down six answers, using different modal verbs, which give an explanation for or opinion about your colleague's absence.

Unit 14

Work vocabulary: Project management

1 Match each verb (1–7) with a noun or noun phrase (a–g).

1	submit	a	research
2	get the	b	a proposal
3	work out	c	results
4	miss	d	track
5	keep on	e	a schedule
6	carry out	f	a deadline
7	evaluate	g	go-ahead

2 Put these terms into groups under the three headings.

> product testing   contingency plan   quality control   cost-benefit analysis
> aims and objectives   SWOT analysis   project meeting   GANTT chart
> monitoring and controlling

Management tool	Internal planning	Quality management

Professional communication: Negotiating 1 – Stating positive expectations and preferences

3 Read these comments from a negotiation over a commercial property development. Complete the sentences using words from the box.

> common ground   put forward   confident   prioritise
> alternatives   way to look at this   prefer

PE = positive expectations   SP = stating preferences
SA = stating alternatives

1 (PE) We are .... we'll reach a good solution for all parties.
2 (PE) We think there is a lot of .... between us.
3 (SP) We'd .... to see a modern and innovative design.
4 (SP) Because it's so important, we'd like to .... energy efficiency.
5 (SA) There are a couple of .... we'd like to ....
6 (SA) Another .... is to look at similar projects in other places.

Over to you

Think of a project you have been involved in. Write a paragraph describing the key stages in the project using some of the words in exercises 1 and 2.

General communication: Complaining

1 Unscramble the letters in brackets to make a word which will complete an expression you can use when you want to complain.

1 I want to make a .... (pantloimc)
2 There's a .... with the shower. (melborp)
3 It's .... and I'd like you to do something about it. (kornbe)
4 I'd like my .... back. (yomen)
5 I really think I deserve better .... than this. (mtertaten)
6 I think I am entitled to a full .... on this. (breate)
7 Yes, I'd be .... with that. (distifsae)
8 Thank you for dealing with this so .... (mylptrop)
9 I .... the way you've handled this. (patpaiceer)

2 Use some of the scrambled words above to complete these sentences.

1 I really .... everything you've done for us.
2 I'm not at all happy with the .... we've received.
3 I wish to register a formal ....
4 I think you could have reacted more .... than you have done.
5 You told me that we would get our .... back if we weren't totally satisfied.
6 I should get a tax .... this year.

General vocabulary: Consumer issues

3 Match words from the columns to make phrases about consumer issues.

1 best	5 full	a goods	e protection
2 consumer	6 excessive	b scare	f adviser
3 small	7 food	c print	g rebate
4 faulty	8 financial	d charges	h buy

4 Match what the businesses say (1–5) with the customer descriptions (a–e).

1 Someone has said he's not happy.   a customer delight
2 We want them always to come to us.   b customer expectations
3 The feedback is getting worse.   c customer loyalty
4 We want them to be more than just   d customer complaint
   satisfied.   e customer dissatisfaction
5 They want better and better service.

Over to you

Write a short letter to a hotel complaining about the quality of the service during your recent stay there.

Unit 16

Grammar: Adverbs – Describing places

1 Read the text and find two examples of each type of adverb: *manner, degree, frequency, attitude* and *place / time* (one each).

Welcome to Dubai

Area The total area of Dubai is approximately 3,900 sq. km.

Economy Today, the UAE is one of the world's wealthiest countries, a land where the oil never stops flowing.

Cultural mix Amazingly, more than 75% of Dubai's inhabitants are expatriates from over 180 countries.

Weather Visitors always enjoy warm sunshine 365 days of the year.

Places of interest The range of attractions is marvellous. In the morning you can watch potters and weavers working carefully to produce wonderful handicrafts. In the afternoon you can wander pleasantly along superb stretches of beach, taking in the views of Dubai's most exclusive luxury hotels, including the famous Burj Al Arab Hotel, shown here. You can also find the Grand Mosque – a famous landmark and place of worship. Interestingly, the city has one of the largest gold markets in the world. You will find everything from ingots to handcrafted jewellery. The place is a must for serious jewellery shoppers. But be careful ... it's seriously expensive.

Grammar: Adverbs – Explaining benefits

2 Read the service guarantees from the Arabia Hotel and put the adverbs in brackets in the right place in each sentence. Sometimes more than one position is possible.

Stay at the Arabia Hotel – where dreams come true

1 We guarantee a tailored experience. (individually, totally)

2 All our rooms are decorated to the highest standards. (tastefully, now)

3 The hotel is located so that guests can explore the sights in the surrounding area. (easily, ideally)

4 Our well-equipped fitness centre with modern gym and two pools is located on the third floor of the hotel. (conveniently, superbly)

5 The refurbished dining room has luxurious decoration. (wonderfully, newly)

6 The service, hospitality and professionalism at the Arabia create an environment where life and dreams can meet. (here, perfectly)

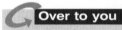

Over to you

Write a short text for a tourist brochure describing a famous place which you have visited. Use a range of adverbs to make the place sound as interesting as possible.

Work vocabulary: Marketing 1

1 Match the definitions (1–8) with the words in the box.

> franchise   promotion   premium brands   spam
> leaflets   marketing mix   positioning   junk mail

1 Advertising that comes on a single sheet of paper telling you about products or promotions
2 Advertising material that you have not asked for that is posted to your home or work address
3 Unwanted advertising emails that come to your computer
4 High priced and high quality products or services
5 A business that trades under a famous brand name and pays for the right to do so
6 The activity which relates a specific set of product characteristics to the needs of specific consumers
7 The combination of management choices which together make up the effort to produce and sell products or services
8 Any activity which is designed to make products or services better known

Professional communication: Presenting 3 – Using visual supports

2 Unscramble the words to make sentences from a presentation describing sales results and forecasts. The first word of each sentence is provided.

1 This ...   shows over graph years increased the last sales five
2 As ...   share our market see can has reached you 10%
3 Now ...   three a at the years forecast the look for next take
4 Clearly, ...   turnover the both profit for positive look very figures and
5 You'll ...   next from figures we that year plan to grow notice these 20%
6 The ...   slide steps final the growth this action to highlights secure

Over to you

Find a magazine or newspaper. Select some visual images – photographs, charts, tables or graphs – and write sentences describing them.

Unit 18

General communication: Persuading

1 Correct one word in each of these sentences.
1 I dishonestly believe you'd enjoy it.
2 You'd really make on with the other guys.
3 Make me show you the brochure.
4 It's across to you, but I'd love you to come.

2 Complete each of these sentences with a verb from the box.
1 Why don't you .... it a try?
2 I'm sure you'd .... it.
3 Everyone would .... you to come.
4 It would be great to .... you there.
5 Please won't you .... ?
6 Why don't you .... along – just this once?

reconsider
enjoy
love
come
have
give

General vocabulary: Holidays and holiday problems

3 Using the words and phrases below, make eight pairs of words or words and phrases which have similar meanings.
Example: robbery – theft

| robbery   safe   harass   unaccompanied   single   valuables |
| wallet   assault   deposit box   jewellery   pester   pickpocket |
| theft   money belt   bag snatcher   mugging |

4 Complete the holiday phrases in these sentences.
1 Did you h_ _ _ a g_ _ _ holiday?
2 When are you g_ _ _ _ o_ holiday this year?
3 To b_ _ _ your dream holiday now, call this Freephone number.
4 Our US budget holiday d_ _ _ _ _ _ _ _ _ _ include New York, Washington, San Francisco and Miami.
5 He's done very well. He has a house in London and holiday h_ _ _ _ in Tuscany and the South of France.
6 Cycling, caving, walking and climbing are just some of the range of a_ _ _ _ _ _ _ holidays we have on offer.
7 When do the schools b_ _ _ _ u_ for their holiday this summer?
8 For more information, call now for our full colour holiday b_ _ _ _ _ _ _ .

 Over to you

Write sentences about holidays and holiday problems using some of the words in exercise 3.

Grammar: Passive – Profiling organisations and products

1 *Time* – the first news magazine Complete this conversation about *Time* with the correct passive form of each verb.

A: So, who founded *Time* magazine?

B: It (1) .... (found) by two men, Henry Luce and Briton Hadden, in 1923.

A: And what was the concept behind it?

B: The magazine (2) .... (write) to be read in an hour so that busy people could keep themselves informed about what was happening easily.

A: (3) .... (it / read) every week by many people in China?

B: I don't know the actual sales figures but there's an Asian edition which (4) .... (base) in Hong Kong.

A: Who (5) .... (*Time* / own)?

B: Since 1989, the magazine (6) .... (own) by Time Warner.

A: Can you tell me about the *Time* 'Person of the Year'? I know the magazine nominates a person with the biggest news effect.

B: Yes, that's a very popular feature. In fact, the person of the year for this year (7) .... (currently / decide). But no decision yet!

A: When (8) .... (the person / will / name)?

B: It (9) .... (should / announce) in early December.

Grammar: Passive – Reporting business news

2 Complete the newsletter headlines using the words in brackets with the verb in the passive.

1 (an average / five working days / per employee / lose / due / sickness / last year) ....

2 (current workforce / cut by 5% / since / beginning / year)
....

3 (new IT network / currently / install)
....

4 (Plastics Division / totally / reorganise / at / end / next year)
....

5 (greater improvements / quality / must / achieve / by / end / next year)
....

6 (the company / say / to be / discussion with / a rival / about / merger)
....

Over to you

Write a short report describing a past, present or future piece of business news in your organisation using the passive tenses studied in this unit.

Unit 20

Work vocabulary: Marketing 2

1 Match (1–10) with (a–j) to form common marketing collocations.

1 mass ....   5 database ....   8 customer .... surveys
2 brand ....   6 marketing ....   9 competitor ....
3 after-sales ....   7 brand ....   10 consumer ....
4 market ....

a tools	b image	c name	d service	e marketing
f satisfaction	g needs	h research	i analysis	j mix

2 Complete the text using phrases from exercise **1**.

For business-to-business marketing, a (1) .... approach is a waste of time. But for consumer marketing it is important to carry out effective (2) .... This means properly identifying (3) .... and developing products to meet them. For consumer goods you need the right (4) .... of product, price, promotion and place. All organisations should carry out good after-sales studies including (5) .... Organisations should develop good (6) .... to help understand the market. This should include (7) .... Organisations should also try to develop a strong (8) .... , because a (9) .... can be the organisation's most important asset. Finally, remember that the quality of the (10) .... is important, or customers will choose a competitor next time.

Professional communication: Meetings 2 – Teleconferencing

3 You are taking part in a teleconference. What do you say in these situations?
   1 Introduce yourself and say where you are calling from.
   2 You did not hear what Daniel Li just said.
   3 You want some information sent by email. Ask Lorraine Perez.
   4 You think someone has just said $450,000. Check that.
   5 You have a bad connection and can't hear properly.
   6 You have to leave in a few minutes as you have another meeting.
   7 Ask Ms Perez to summarise the discussion so far.
   8 Interrupt your friend Mario Castellano.
   9 Ask Ms Perez to organise another teleconference.
   10 Tell her you think this has been a very good meeting.

Over to you

Think of your own organisation or an organisation you know well. Write a paragraph describing aspects of its marketing using some of the phrases from this unit.

General communication: Dealing with people who are difficult to understand

1 Unscramble the words to make sentences you can use to deal with people who are difficult to understand. Two of them are questions.
 1 you please can that explain
 2 but don't said what I'm just sorry I understand you've
 3 much know that computers don't assume I about that
 4 what you do exactly talk through me to can

General vocabulary: Books and reading

2 Choose the right sequencing phrases to tell the story of *The Curious Incident of the Dog in the Night-time* by **Mark Haddon.**
 1 *At first | First of all* Christopher finds a dead dog in his next-door neighbour's garden.
 2 *Second of all | Next* we learn something about Christopher's life as an autistic child and his life with his father. Christopher's father has told him that his mother is dead.
 3 *At first | First* he doesn't know who killed the dog.
 4 *But then | After* he decides to do some detective work to find the killer.
 5 *Afterwards | After that* he finds some letters from his mother and learns that she is not dead after all but is alive and living in London.
 6 *Thus | So* he decides to go to London with his pet rat to find her.
 7 It is a nightmare journey for him to travel on his own to a strange place but *at last | at least* he finds his mother.
 8 *Finally | The last thing is*, his father comes to London and ... (if you want to know how the book ends, you'll have to read it!).

3 Put these types of book into groups under the two headings.

| poetry | biography | short story | current affairs | novel | cookery |
| historical novel | crime | philosophy | history | drama | travel |

Fiction	Non-fiction

Over to you
Briefly write the story of one of your favourite novels and explain why you like it.

Unit 22

Grammar: Revision of first and second conditional; third conditional – Explaining consequences

1 Complete these sentences using the correct form of the verb in brackets.

1 Yes, but if we .... (buy) new software as you suggest, it would be very expensive.

2 If you .... (train) her properly, she wouldn't have hurt herself.

3 If you .... (have) time this afternoon, I'll show you around the city.

4 I .... (not / lose) the data if I'd saved the files just five minutes before.

5 If this .... (happen) again, I'm sorry but I'll have to report the matter to Finance.

6 I .... (speak) to your manager about the problem if I were you.

2 Which of the sentences above contains (a) an offer of help, (b) a threat and (c) advice?

Grammar: Revision of third conditional – Expressing regret

3 Complete these *if* sentences, which comment on business mistakes made in the past, using the words in brackets.

1 I didn't prepare the presentation properly so it didn't go very well.
If I'd prepared .... (*prepare | go well*)

2 We priced the product far too high and so sales were very poor.
If .... (*price lower | be better*)

3 I forgot to email the offer in time so we lost the business.
If .... (*remember | got the business*)

4 I didn't tell my client I was a vegetarian so I couldn't eat the dinner he'd prepared.
If .... (*inform | prepare vegetarian food*)

5 I wasn't able to get a flight to New York so I didn't make the conference.
If .... (*get a flight | attended the conference*)

6 We spent too much money in the first six months so we couldn't afford the workshop.
If .... (*spend less | could afford the workshop*)

Over to you

Write five sentences describing things which didn't go well for you or your organisation in the past. Then write down five third conditional sentences describing how things could have been different.

Work vocabulary: Meetings and conferences

1 **Complete these sentences with words from the box.**

> minutes   details   purpose   agenda   equipment   apology   on time

1 Most formal meetings have a written ....
2 The most important thing about a meeting is that it has a clear
   ....
3 The organisers of the meeting should send out .... in good
   time.
4 If you cannot attend a meeting, it is often a good idea to send an
   ....
5 A formal meeting usually has someone writing a record of what is
   said or agreed, called the ....
6 Meetings should start and end ....
7 It's important to check that all the .... needed for the
   meeting is available and working.

Professional communication: Negotiating 2 – Bargaining and reaching a compromise

2 **Write sentences for each step in the negotiation below about hiring a venue for a one-day conference meeting for 50 participants.**

Venue representative	Organiser
Offer a main hall and two smaller rooms plus audio-visual equipment for $5,000	
	Ask how much refreshments are – coffee and tea (twice) plus lunch
$20 per delegate ($1,000)	
	Ask for the entire package for $4,500
Reject this – offer $5,500	
	Suggest you will supply audio-visual equipment and pay only $4,500
Agree	
	Summarise the agreement

Over to you

Think about the last time you organised or attended a meeting. Write a paragraph describing the organisation of the meeting and what you did. What happened before, during and after the meeting?

Unit 24

General communication: Dealing with conflict

1 Complete these sentences which you can use to deal with conflict.

1 I really am s............................ .
2 I g...................... I should have t........................ to leave the meeting earlier.
3 It would be a real p........................ to stop just because I got delayed once.
4 Try and s............................ it from my p............................ of v............................ .
5 You have to a............................ that it's not always possible.
6 I'm glad that you a............................ my p............................ .

2 Christine is talking about the conflict she has with a work colleague. Complete the advice she gives herself with verbs from the box.

| accept | agree | give | make | knows |

1 I must try to .... things better between us.
2 But I mustn't .... in to his demands.
3 I must make sure that he .... what I think.
4 I mustn't .... too much pressure.
5 And I mustn't .... to do things that aren't possible.

General vocabulary: Your education

3 Complete each sentence with a word or phrase from the box. Put the verbs in the right tense.

| apply | place | grant | study | high | secondary | Master's |
| graduate | subject | primary | school leaver's certificate | degree |

1 My parents moved a lot when I was young so I went to ....
  school in France.
2 Then I went to .... school in Germany.
3 Then I went to a .... school for 16- to 18-year-olds in Sweden.
4 I did my international baccalaureate there – that's a kind of ....
5 Then I .... to university in the UK.
6 I got a .... at the University of Leeds to ....
  mechanical engineering.
7 But after one year I decided to change to another ....
8 After three years I .... with a good second class honours
  .... in mathematics.
9 I thought about doing a .... in business administration.
10 But I couldn't get a .... so I decided to get a job instead.

 Over to you

Write a few sentences about the educational system in your country.

Grammar: Future reference – Finalising travel plans

1 Complete the conversation by choosing the correct future form.

A: Alex, I don't have our flight details for next week. (1) *Are we flying |
Are we going to fly* on Wednesday morning or in the afternoon?

B: The flight (2) *leaves | is going to leave* at 10 in the morning, which
means (3) *we're going to land | we'll be landing* at 1.30 local time.

A: Good. (4) *I'm going to | I'll* book a taxi to the airport for us for 7.30.

B: I think (5) *we're going to have | we're having* a good time in Milan.

A: Absolutely.

B: (6) *Do you | Are you going to* arrange your meeting with Mauro Ronzoni
for Thursday?

A: Yes, that's the plan.

B: But don't book any restaurants. (7) *I'm going to book | I book* everything
when we arrive.

A: OK. See you on Wednesday morning. Remember, the taxi (8) *leaves | is
going to leave* at 7.30.

B: Don't worry. (9) *I'll | I'm going to* be ready.

Grammar: Future reference – Describing future arrangements

2 Make sentences using the future continuous to complete the dialogues.

1 A: Jo, when .... (you / arrive) tomorrow because I need to
plan our meeting?
   B: I should be here by about 2 o'clock.

2 A: Will my computer be ready for tomorrow morning?
   B: No, I .... (still / repair) it. You should have it by early afternoon.

3 A: Are you on holiday as from tomorrow?
   B: Yes! This time tomorrow I .... (relax) on the beach.

4 A: If you bump into Hans, can you tell him to call me?
   B: Sure. I .... (see) him after lunch so I can ask him then.

5 A: Have we received that late invoice payment from Tectronics yet?
   B: Not yet. I think we .... (still / wait) this time next year unless
we threaten them with legal action.

**3 In which of the sentences in exercise 2 can you substitute the present
continuous to express the idea of a fixed future arrangement?**

Over to you

Write sentences saying what you will be doing this time next week, next month and
next year.

Unit 26

Work vocabulary: Public relations

1 Match each word on the left with a word on the right which has a similar meaning.

1	air, land and water	a	stakeholders
2	plan	b	transparency
3	openness	c	welfare
4	ethical	d	responsibility
5	accountability	e	strategy
6	people involved or affected	f	moral
7	health and happiness	g	environment

2 Complete the newspaper report with words from the right-hand column in exercise 1.

The director of public relations for the Corporations Guild, Sir Clifford Goodman, said at the society's annual general meeting in London yesterday that the corporate sector must connect more closely with the public. 'We have an absolute (1) .... to think about the consequences of what we do,' he told delegates to the meeting. He said that the (2) .... in a business were not only the employees and the customers, but also the wider community. 'Of course, the (3) .... of staff is important, but we also have a (4) .... obligation to think about the (5) .... as well.' He ended his address by stressing that every organisation should develop a PR (6) .... that is based on (7) .... and honesty.

Professional communication: Meetings 3 – Summarising and closing

3 Suggest sentences for the end of a project meeting based on these prompts.

1 Indicate that there is not much time left (it's almost 6 o'clock).
2 List three main conclusions from the meeting (the project is on schedule, within costs, and will be extremely successful).
3 Emphasise a point from the meeting (there's still a lot of work to do).
4 Ask if there is anything important left to add.
5 Give a positive message about the meeting.
6 Suggest a future meeting (in a fortnight).
7 Close the meeting.

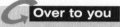**Over to you**

Write sentences summarising the conclusions of a meeting you have been involved in or summarising the speech made by Sir Clifford Goodman in exercise 2.

General communication: Giving feedback

1 Complete each sentence with a verb from the box to make expressions for giving feedback to someone who wants to improve his/her presentation technique. Remember to put the verb into the right tense.

work	like	help	find	go

1 How do you think it .... on the whole?
2 I particularly .... the way you remembered to ...
3 What did you .... most difficult about it?
4 Is there anything else you should .... on for next time?
5 I'm sure breathing properly can ....

2 Match the advice for giving feedback (1–5) with examples of feedback about a presentation (a–e).

1 Give focused praise first.
2 Get the other person to talk about his/her performance.
3 Focus on what you're being positive about.
4 Identify obstacles.
5 Define an action plan.

a Were you happy with it?
b The opening was very effective.
c What are you going to do to get that right next time?
d What's stopping you from getting the timing right?
e The first slide was very effective in getting the audience involved.

General vocabulary: Personal finance

3 Match words from the columns to make personal finance phrases.

1 student	5 investment	a price	e repayment
2 early	6 credit	b dispenser	f loan
3 state	7 cash	c card	g advice
4 debt	8 share	d retirement	h pension

4 Put these words into groups under the four headings.

plan	health	account	fund	statement	overdraft	affairs
situation	accident	adviser	contribution	travel		

bank ~	pension ~	~ insurance	financial ~

Over to you

Write sentences using the expressions in exercise **3** *or* write your own golden rules for personal financial management.

Unit 28

Grammar: Direct and reported speech – Reporting feedback

1 Your project team recently went to America to visit a subsidiary. Report the team's feedback by changing the direct speech to reported speech. More than one answer is possible.

1 'It was really interesting to see how my American colleagues worked.'
Petra said ....

2 'Can I discuss the next exchange visit as soon as possible?'
Jean-Marc wanted to know ....

3 'They have far fewer holidays than us!'
Anna Maria commented ....

4 'Our US colleagues were extremely open and welcoming.'
Jorge stressed ....

5 'When is the team going back?'
Claudia asked ....

6 'Our US colleagues are working on very interesting projects at the moment.' Antonio thought ....

Grammar: Direct and reported speech – Reporting and simplifying what others say

2 Here are some examples of direct speech between a project leader and a team member. Match each reporting verb (1–8) with a sentence in direct speech (a–h).

| 1 suggest | 2 warn | 3 insist | 4 remind | 5 ask | 6 praise | 7 admit | 8 invite |

a 'Well done. It was a great job to finish the Telco project on time.'
b 'It would be good if you could come to dinner on Monday.'
c 'Is there anything that you want to give me feedback about?'
d 'No arguments! Go and see a doctor today about your headaches.'
e 'Remember that you need to call Sam tomorrow.'
f 'I accept that maybe I didn't give you enough support last year.'
g 'Why don't you apply for the vacant sales management position?'
h 'Don't tell Mr Dobson how you feel. He can't be trusted.'

3 Now imagine someone said sentences (a–h) to you. Use the reporting verbs (1–8) to change and simplify the sentences into reported speech beginning 'He/She ...' More than one answer is possible.

Over to you

Watch an English-language television news programme (business or general) or look at a news website. Write down in reported speech five questions asked by news journalists and the five corresponding answers.

Work vocabulary: Legal issues

1 Complete each sentence (1–8) with a word from the box. Then match each sentence with one of the pictures (a–h).

1 Eva claimed .... for her injuries.
2 The company went .... last year.
3 We have registered the ....
4 The company was taken to ....
5 He was found .... and sent to prison.
6 They agreed to set up a ....
7 Megacorp made several ....
8 The band signed a .... with a recording company.

contract	guilty
bankrupt	joint venture
compensation	trademark
court	acquisitions

Professional communication: Writing 2 – Clear writing

2 Read three examples of unclear writing (A–C). Rewrite them as emails in less than 20 words each, making only the most important point(s). Choose a subject line for each email.

A I was wondering about something. It would be good to know – if you are happy about this – could you let me know what time you might arrive on Thursday – because I have to go out in the morning – but I will be back whenever you arrive – I don't have to go out – I mean it's not urgent.

B The conclusions of our enquiry are more or less as you would expect. In fact we were not surprised by the conclusion. After a long study of our experience over the years, we think we should try to arrange for a joint venture – a long-term agreement – to develop some programmes with Zillessen Inc.

C The question is should we buy the property. There are one or two problems. First of all, it is not clear from our lawyer who the owner of the property is. Also the condition is not very good. The local authority is also not happy about it becoming a commercial property – it was a school before. We think therefore it is not a good idea to buy the place and in fact I don't think we should spend any more time on it – you may think from this we are not interested in it.

 **Over to you**

Find a news story in a newspaper. Read it and then summarise it in about 20 words.

Unit 30

General communication: Getting important messages across

1 Complete these ideas for getting messages across with a verb.

1 .... the right moment.
2 .... the importance of the message.
3 .... sure the person you want to talk to will listen and knows it's important.
4 .... the message a heading.
5 .... the meaning clear.
6 .... your story to life.
7 .... fuzzy language.
8 .... about where, who, when and what.

General vocabulary: Personal development

2 Do you know the *English365* action plan for developing your English? Fill the gaps in these sentences.

1 Think about .... you want to learn.
2 Think about .... it is to learn English. If it is important for you and your job, you will give it a lot of time.
3 Decide .... you can give to your English. You can learn a lot in five or ten minutes per day. Little and often is best.
4 Think about .... you want to learn. Have an objective for each day, each week and each month.
5 Think about .... you learn. For example, do you like to hear new language or to write it down or to see it on the page?
6 .... your work for the day, the week and the month to come.
7 .... yourself. Give yourself presents when you reach goals.
8 .... yourself .... and speaking English well. This 'mental modelling' can be good for your learning.
9 Keep a .... Good learners think about their learning.
10 .... your work. We often don't learn something the first time we do it. We often have to do something three or more times before we can do it well.

3 Remember the golden rules for language learning. Fill the gaps again.

1 .... what you are going to learn. Have clear goals.
2 .... what you are learning.
3 .... what you have learnt.

Over to you

If you had problems with exercises **2** or **3**, look again at pages 6–7. Look again too at your Better language learning notes on pages 8–11. Are you following your plan?

Answer key to Practice exercises

to Practice exercises

Unit 1

Grammar: Present simple and continuous; present perfect simple and continuous – Introducing an organisation

1 1 organises 2 has been providing / has provided 3 owns
4 has received 5 are expanding 6 lets 7 have been developing

Grammar: Present simple and continuous; present perfect simple and continuous – Keeping small talk going

2 1 are you staying 2 have you been coming 3 have you been
4 do you come / have you been coming 5 have never been 6 run
7 do you do

Unit 2

Work vocabulary: Managing organisations

1 1 responsibility 2 leadership 3 by example 4 creative
5 mistakes 6 experience 7 channels 8 sort out

Professional communication: Writing 1 – Emails and register

2 Email 1
1 a 2 c 3 a 4 b 5 a 6 c 7 b 8 c 9 a 10 a
Hi Alex,
You really shouldn't be working. I thought you were having the day off. Why don't you forget all about work when you're not here? Sorry, I can't help, I don't know what Jack decided. You could ring him on his mobile. Or maybe if you want I'll tell him to call you. See you soon.
Your first name only
Email 2
1 b 2 b 3 b 4 a 5 c 6 b 7 c 8 a 9 c 10 b
Dear Mr Nicoletti,
I was pleased to get your message. It would be good if we can meet when you come to London. Please let me know the exact dates of your visit. Will your colleague Ms Costanza be with you? Perhaps we can organise a half-day meeting. Do let me know if I can send you any information to help you before then. Looking forward to hearing from you.
Best wishes,
Your first name and your family name

Unit 3

General communication: Getting started

1 1 Hello, I don't know anyone here.
2 Do you mind if I talk to you?
3 Excuse me, is anyone sitting here?
4 So you work in the hospital. What do you do there?

5 I've always wanted to meet a film producer.
6 Do you work / live here or are you just a visitor?
7 I'm in computers.
8 What do you think of the food?

2 a 6   b 3   c 7   d 2

General vocabulary: Newspaper headlines

3 talks – discussions
envoy – diplomat
poll – survey of public opinion
coup – change of government
blaze – fire
aid – help
key – important
go-ahead – approval
jet – aeroplane
halt – stop
head – lead
blast – explosion

Unit 4

Grammar: Verb grammar – Explaining benefits
1 1 to take   2 not to   3 you   4 you   5 you to   6 visit   7 to buy   8 you

Grammar: Verb grammar – Talking about products
2 1 b   2 a   3 a   4 b   5 a   6 b   7 b   8 a

Unit 5

Work vocabulary: Financial planning and control
1 1 borrow   2 lend   3 charge   4 invest in   5 prepare a budget
6 break even   7 schedule   8 forecast   9 compile   10 control
11 overrun   12 assess

Professional communication: Presenting 1 – Progress reports
2 1 d   2 c   3 a   4 g   5 b   6 e

Unit 6

General communication: Building rapport
1 1 b   2 e   3 d   4 c   5 a

General vocabulary: Current affairs and economic issues
2 1 privatisation   2 natural environment   3 recreation facilities
4 health services   5 traffic congestion   6 housing
7 full employment   8 waste disposal

3	Verb	Person noun	General noun	Adjective
	consume	CONSUMER	consumption consumerism	x
	economise	economist	economy economics	ECONOMIC economical
	x	environmentalist	ENVIRONMENT	environmental
	politicise	politician	politics	POLITICAL
	educate	educator	EDUCATION	educational

Unit 7

Grammar: Past simple, past continuous and past perfect simple – Describing personal history

1 1 came   2 had inherited   3 had helped   4 decided   5 became
6 were handing in / handed in   7 skipping / skipped
8 formed   9 arose   10 began

Grammar: Past simple, past continuous and past perfect simple – Describing past experiences

2 1 was installing   2 was   3 had to   4 crashed   5 was setting up
6 turned on   7 discovered   8 had managed   9 had finished
10 did not / didn't have to

Unit 8

Work vocabulary: Politics

1 1 strategic partnerships   2 stakeholders   3 Chamber of Commerce
4 global citizenship   5 city council   6 health authority
7 trade unions

Professional communication: Presenting 2 – Structuring

2 *Suggested answers*
1 Hello, everyone.
2 The title of my short presentation is 'Internet marketing – Developing e-prospects'.
3 The talk is in three parts.
4 I'll begin with some background – talking about our overall marketing approach. Then I'll talk about how we use the web now and highlight current strengths and weaknesses. Finally, I want to say something about some new initiatives.
5 There'll be time for any questions and discussion afterwards.
6 So, let's begin then with the background.
7 That's all on our general approach to marketing. Now I'll move on to talking about our current web use and the strengths and weaknesses.

Unit 9

General communication: Listening

1 1 That's really interesting.
2 Tell me what happened then.
3 Where exactly did you go? / Where did you go exactly?
4 That sounds really wonderful.
5 I see what you mean.
6 And how did you feel about that?
7 That must have been very difficult.
8 It sounds as if you had a great time.
2 1 c 2 e 3 d 4 a 5 b

General vocabulary: The weather

3 1 spells 2 showers 3 wind 4 breezes 5 temperatures 6 rain
7 gale, ground 8 forecast

Unit 10

Grammar: Multi-word verbs – Giving opinions about technology

1 a 2 b 3 c 2 d 1 e 2 f 4 g 3 h 2

Grammar: Multi-word verbs – Discussing project problems

2 1 We have run up against a few problems during the software installation.
2 I'm not sure when we will get round the problems.
3 This means putting off installation / putting installation off until next year.
4 I hope you can live with this.
5 We will try to make up the time / make the time up later in the project.
6 I'll work out the cost / work the cost out of any delays.
7 I'm confident we can stick to the initial budget.
8 If you want to talk about this, please call me.

Unit 11

Work vocabulary: Quality

1 1 e 2 a 3 f 4 b 5 c 6 d
2 1 professional, skilled / specialist 2 training programmes / procedures
3 automated systems 4 visual checks 5 customer feedback
6 efficiency

Professional communication: Meetings 1 – Listening and helping understanding

3 1 slowly and clearly 2 Repeat or summarise 3 written report or notes
4 keep to the point 5 first, then, next, finally
6 There are three points 7 keep eye contact

Unit 12

General communication: Dealing with 'no'
1 1 minute, through   2 afraid   3 honest, hoping, positive
4 disappointed   5 way, look   6 find, solution   7 affect   8 help
2 *Suggested answers*
a 8   b 3   c 4   d 5

General vocabulary: TV and TV programmes
3 1 channel   2 individual performance   3 plot   4 listings magazine
5 rating   6 recording   7 scheduling   8 repeat   9 satellite

Unit 13

Grammar: Modal verbs to express certainty – Discussing office news
1 1 must   2 should   3 could   4 must   5 might have taken   6 should

Grammar: Modal verbs to express certainty – Discussing possibilities
2 1 should appoint   2 might / could / may be   3 must / will have had
4 might / may / could have been   5 may / might / could be
6 won't / can't be   7 will have received   8 shouldn't / won't be

Unit 14

Work vocabulary: Project management
1 1 b   2 g   3 e   4 f   5 d   6 a   7 c
2 Management tool: cost-benefit analysis, SWOT analysis, GANTT chart
Internal planning: contingency plan, aims and objectives, project meeting
Quality management: product testing, quality control, monitoring and
controlling

Professional communication: Negotiating 1 – Stating positive expectations and preferences
3 1 confident   2 common ground   3 prefer   4 prioritise
5 alternatives, put forward   6 way to look at this

Unit 15

General communication: Complaining
1 1 complaint   2 problem   3 broken   4 money   5 treatment
6 rebate   7 satisfied   8 promptly   9 appreciate
2 1 appreciate   2 treatment   3 complaint   4 promptly
5 money   6 rebate

General vocabulary: Consumer issues
3 1 h   2 e   3 c   4 a   5 g   6 d   7 b   8 f
4 1 d   2 c   3 e   4 a   5 b

Unit 16

Grammar: Adverbs – Describing places
1 manner: carefully, pleasantly
degree: approximately, seriously
frequency: never, always
attitude: amazingly, interestingly
place: here
time: today

Grammar: Adverbs – Explaining benefits
2 1 We guarantee a totally individually tailored experience.
2 (Now) All our rooms are (now) tastefully decorated to the highest standards (now).
3 The hotel is ideally located so that guests can (easily) explore (easily) the sights in the surrounding area (easily).
4 Our superbly well-equipped fitness centre with modern gym and two pools is (conveniently) located (conveniently) on the third floor of the hotel.
5 The newly refurbished dining room has wonderfully luxurious decoration.
6 The service, hospitality and professionalism here at the Arabia create an environment where life and dreams can meet perfectly.

Unit 17

Work vocabulary: Marketing 1
1 1 leaflets   2 junk mail   3 spam   4 premium brands   5 franchise
6 positioning   7 marketing mix   8 promotion

Professional communication: Presenting 3 – Using visual supports
2 *Suggested answers*
1 This graph shows increased sales over the last five years.
2 As you can see, our market share has reached 10%.
3 Now take a look at the forecast for the next three years.
4 Clearly, the figures for both turnover and profit look very positive.
5 You'll notice from these figures that we plan to grow 20% next year.
6 The final slide highlights the action steps to secure this growth.

Unit 18

General communication: Persuading
1 1 I honestly believe you'd enjoy it.
2 You'd really get on with the other guys.
3 Let me show you the brochure.
4 It's up to you, but I'd love you to come.
2 1 give   2 enjoy   3 love   4 have   5 reconsider   6 come

General vocabulary: Holidays and holiday problems

3 robbery – theft   safe – deposit box   harass – pester
unaccompanied – single   valuables – jewellery   wallet – money belt
assault – mugging   pickpocket – bag snatcher

4 1 have, good   2 going on   3 book   4 destinations   5 homes
6 activity   7 break up   8 brochure

Unit 19

Grammar: Passive – Profiling organisations and products

1 1 was founded   2 was written   3 Is it read   4 is based
5 is *Time* owned by   6 has been owned   7 is currently being decided
8 will the person be named   9 should be announced

Grammar: Passive – Reporting business news

2 1 An average of five working days per employee was lost due to sickness
last year.
2 The current workforce has been cut by 5% since the beginning of the
year.
3 A new IT network is currently being installed.
4 The Plastics Division will be totally reorganised at the end of next
year.
5 Greater improvements in quality must be achieved by the end of next
year.
6 The company is said to be in discussion with a rival about a merger.

Unit 20

Work vocabulary: Marketing 2

1 1 e   2 c / b   3 d   4 h   5 a   6 j   7 b / c   8 f   9 i   10 g

2 1 mass marketing   2 market research   3 consumer needs
4 marketing mix   5 customer satisfaction surveys   6 database tools
7 competitor analysis   8 brand image   9 brand name
10 after-sales service

Professional communication: Meetings 2 – Teleconferencing

3 *Suggested answers*
1 Hello. My name's X and I'm calling from Y.
2 Sorry, Mr Li. I didn't hear what you said. Can you repeat it?
3 Ms Perez, please can you send me some information by email?
4 Did you say $450,000?
5 I'm sorry. I have a bad connection and I can't hear properly.
6 Unfortunately, I have to leave in a few minutes. I've got to go to
another meeting.
7 Excuse me, Ms Perez. Could you summarise the discussion so far,
please?
8 Sorry, Mario, can I interrupt you? I just want to say ...
9 Ms Perez, is it possible to organise another teleconference?
10 I think this has been a very good meeting. Thank you.

Unit 21

General communication: Dealing with people who are difficult to understand

1 1 Can you explain that, please? / Please can you explain that?
  2 I'm sorry but I don't understand what you've just said.
  3 Assume that I don't know that much about computers.
  4 Can you talk me through what to do exactly / exactly what to do?

General vocabulary: Books and reading

2 1 First of all 2 Next 3 At first 4 But then 5 After that 6 So
  7 at last 8 Finally

3 Fiction: poetry, short story, novel, historical novel, crime, drama
  Non-fiction: biography, current affairs, cookery, philosophy, history,
  travel

Unit 22

Grammar: Revision of first and second conditional; third conditional –
Explaining consequences

1 1 bought 2 had trained 3 have 4 wouldn't have lost 5 happens
  6 would speak

2 3 a 5 b 6 c

Grammar: Revision of third conditional – Expressing regret

3 *Suggested answers*
  1 If I'd prepared the presentation properly, it would have gone well.
  2 If we'd priced the product lower, sales would have been better.
  3 If I'd remembered to email the offer in time, we would have got the
   business.
  4 If I had informed my client, he would have prepared vegetarian food.
  5 If I'd been able to get a flight, I would have attended the conference.
  6 If we'd spent less money, we could have afforded the workshop.

Unit 23

Work vocabulary: Meetings and conferences

1 1 agenda 2 purpose 3 details 4 apology 5 minutes
  6 on time 7 equipment

Professional communication: Negotiating 2 – Bargaining and reaching a
compromise

2 *Suggested answers*
  VENUE REPRESENTATIVE: We can offer you a main hall and two smaller
   rooms, plus audio-visual equipment for $5,000.
  ORGANISER: How much would refreshments be, for example coffee and
   tea in the morning and afternoon, plus lunch?
  V: That would cost $20 per delegate, so $1,000 in total.
  O: Well, what about the entire package for $4,500?
  V: No, sorry. We can't do that. We could suggest $5,500.
  O: No, but as a compromise, what if we supply all the audio-visual
   equipment and pay only $4,500?

V: I see. Well, that's OK.

O: Right, so to summarise, we'll have a one-day conference for 50 participants, with one main room and two smaller rooms. We'll also have lunch plus coffee and tea in the morning and afternoon. There'll be no equipment, because we'll provide that. The total fee will be $4,500. OK?

V: Yes, we agree to that. Thank you.

Unit 24

General communication: Dealing with conflict
1 1 sorry 2 guess, tried 3 pity 4 see, point, view 5 agree
6 accept, point
2 1 make 2 give 3 knows 4 accept 5 agree

General vocabulary: Your education
3 1 primary 2 secondary 3 high 4 school leaver's certificate
5 applied 6 place, study 7 subject 8 graduated, degree
9 Master's 10 grant

Unit 25

Grammar: Future reference – Finalising travel plans
1 1 Are we flying 2 leaves 3 we'll be landing 4 I'll
5 we're going to have 6 Are you going to 7 I'm going to book
8 is going to leave 9 I'll

Grammar: Future reference – Describing future arrangements
2 1 will you be arriving 2 will still be repairing 3 will be relaxing
4 will be seeing 5 will still be waiting
3 1, 4

Unit 26

Work vocabulary: Public relations
1 1 g 2 e 3 b 4 f 5 d 6 a 7 c
2 1 responsibility 2 stakeholders 3 welfare 4 moral
5 environment 6 strategy 7 transparency

Professional communication: Meetings 3 – Summarising and closing
3 *Suggested answers*
1 We need to finish – there isn't much time left – it's almost 6 o'clock.
2 I'd like to sum up. There are three main conclusions from the meeting. First, the project is on schedule. Secondly, we are within costs. And finally, we are confident that it will be extremely successful.
3 I would like to emphasise that there is still a lot of work to do.
4 Is there anything important left to add?
5 So, it's been a very positive and useful meeting. Thank you to everyone.
6 What about another meeting? Shall we meet again in a fortnight?
7 That's it, then. Thank you.

Unit 27

General communication: Giving feedback
1 1 went   2 liked   3 find   4 work   5 help
2 1 b   2 a   3 e   4 d   5 c

General vocabulary: Personal finance
3 1 f / c   2 d   3 h   4 e   5 g   6 c   7 b   8 a
4 bank: account, statement, overdraft
pension: plan, fund, contribution
insurance: health, accident, travel
financial: affairs, situation, adviser (statement)

Unit 28

Grammar: Direct and reported speech – Reporting feedback
1 1 Petra said (that) it was / had been really interesting to see how
her/our American colleagues work / worked.
2 Jean-Marc wanted to know if he could discuss the next exchange visit as
soon as possible.
3 Anna Maria commented that they had far fewer holidays than us / than
we did / had.
Anna Maria commented (that) they have far fewer holidays than us / than
we do / have.
4 Jorge stressed (that) his / our US colleagues were / had been extremely
open and welcoming.
5 Claudia asked when the team is / was going back.
6 Antonio thought our / his US colleagues are / were working on very
interesting projects at the moment.

Grammar: Direct and reported speech – Reporting and simplifying what
others say
2 1 g   2 h   3 d   4 e   5 c   6 a   7 f   8 b
3 *Suggested answers*
a He/She praised me for finishing the Telco project on time.
b He/She invited me to dinner on Monday.
c He/She asked me if I wanted to give him/her any feedback.
d He/She insisted that I see a doctor about my headaches.
e He/She reminded me to call Sam tomorrow.
f He/She admitted not giving me enough support last year.
g He/She suggested applying for the vacant sales management position.
h He/She warned me not to trust Mr Dobson.

Unit 29

Work vocabulary: Legal issues
1 1 compensation d   2 bankrupt c   3 trademark h   4 court g   5 guilty f
6 joint venture a   7 acquisitions b   8 contract e

Professional communication: Writing 2 – Clear writing

2 *Model answers*

A
Subject: Your visit
Alex,
Please tell me when you will arrive.
Best wishes,
Jo

B
Subject: Zillessen Inc.
Carla,
Our recommendation is to create a joint venture for programme development.
Best wishes,
Maria

C
Subject: School property
Charlotte,
Too many problems; we are no longer interested in this property.
Regards,
Tina

Unit 30

General communication: Getting important messages across

1 1 Choose   2 Stress   3 Make   4 Give   5 Make   6 Bring   7 Avoid
8 Talk

General vocabulary: Personal development

2 1 why   2 how important   3 how much time   4 what   5 how   6 Plan
7 Reward   8 Think about, learning well   9 diary   10 Review

3 1 Plan   2 Practise   3 Review

English365

Personal Study Book 3
Audio CD

Contents of the Audio CD

Introduction   63

Part 1 Listening units
  1 Small talk questions about work   64
  2 Small talk questions about organisations and business   65
  3 Small talk questions about holidays   66
  4 Small talk questions about people and places   67
  5 Presenting 1: Progress reports   67
  6 Presenting 2: Structuring   68
  7 Presenting 3: Using visual supports   69
  8 Meetings 1: Listening and helping understanding   70
  9 Meetings 2: Teleconferencing   71
  10 Meetings 3: Summarising and closing   72
  11 Negotiating 1: Stating positive expectations and preferences, suggesting
    alternatives   73
  12 Negotiating 2: Bargaining and reaching a compromise   74

Part 2 Pronunciation
  1 Minimal pairs   76
  2 Using pauses to add impact   76
  3 Emphasising important words   77
  4 Polite disagreement in short answers   77
  5 Stress in word families   77
  6 Adding impact and interest   78
  7 Linking   78
  8 Modal verbs with *have* in third conditional sentences   78
  9 Chunking and pausing   79
  10 Spelling and pronunciation   79

Tapescript: Part 1 Models   80
Answer key to Listening units   84
Learning diaries   88
Track numbers   94

Introduction

Welcome to the *English365* Personal Study Book 3 Audio CD.
There are two parts to the CD.

- Part 1 contains **Listening exercises** to help you practise
  your English on your own. The exercises give you practice
  in some important areas of social and professional
  communication.

- Part 2 contains the **Pronunciation** work from the
  English365 Student's Book 3.

You will need to use the pause button when you listen to the CD.
Practise repeating what you hear as much as possible.

Part 1: Use the pause button to do the exercises.

Part 2: Repeating what you hear will help you to improve your
pronunciation.

Part 1 Listening units

There are 12 Listening units in this part. For each unit there is:
- Model You will hear people talking in different situations. Listen to the CD and answer the questions. You will find the tapescripts for the Models at the back of your book.
- Exercise You will need to look at your book and write down your answers.
- Practice You will practise what you have been doing in the exercise while you listen to the CD.
- Over to you You will answer questions or practise saying sentences while you listen to the CD.

1 Small talk questions about work

MODEL

1 **Julie Mason is a management consultant. Listen to her getting to know Ken Digby, a new team member at a client company, and answer these questions.**
What does Ken do?
When did he join the project team?

2 **Now listen again and note down the questions Julie asks Ken. Pause the recording if you need to.**

EXERCISE

Read the questions below. You will hear answers to eight of the questions. Write down the number of the questions in the order in which they are answered.

1	Job	What do you do exactly?
2	Organisation	Who do you work for?
3	Current workload	Are you very busy at the moment?
4	Current projects	What's your role on this? / What are you working on at the moment?
5	Time with organisation	How long have you worked for ... (*name of organisation*)?
6	Work routine	When do you usually start work in the morning?
7	Started at organisation	When did you join ... (*name of organisation or team*)?
8	Previous job	What did you do before that?
9	Professional history	How long did you work for ... (*name of former organisation*)?
10	Work-related travel	Do you spend a lot of time travelling?
11	Job satisfaction	Do you enjoy ... (*work activity, e.g. travelling, training, etc.*)?
12	Schedule today	Do you have a busy day today?

Now check your answers on page 84.

Now listen and practise asking the questions.

Play the questions again and answer each of the questions about your work.

2 Small talk questions about organisations and business

MODEL

1 Louis Danon is at a conference in France. Listen to him talking to Marina Fusco, a new contact, during a coffee break and answer these questions.
What kind of company does Marina work for?
How many people work for her company?

2 Now listen again and note down the questions Louis asks Marina. Pause the recording if you need to.

EXERCISE

Read the questions below. You will hear answers to eight of the questions. Write down the number of the questions in the order in which they are answered.

1	Type of organisation	Is it a ... (type of organisation)? What does it do?
2	Ownership	Who owns ... (name of organisation)?
3	Turnover	What's the turnover of ... (organisation)?
4	Main competitor	Who's your main competitor?
5	Market	What's the market like at the moment?
6	Products and services	What are your main products and services?
7	Current business	How's business at the moment?
8	Workforce	How many people work for ... (name of organisation)?
9	Location	Where is it based?
10	Founded	When was it founded?
11	Restructuring	Is it reorganising at the moment?
12	Organisation	How is it organised?

Now check your answers on page 84.

PRACTICE

Now listen and practise asking the questions.

OVER TO YOU

Play the questions again and answer each of the questions about your organisation and business.

3 Small talk questions about holidays

MODEL

1 Julie Mason is working in her office. Listen to her talking to Ian
  Harrow and answer these questions.
  Where did Ian go on holiday?
  What did he do during his holiday there?

2 Now listen again and note down Ian's answers to the questions Julie
  asks below. Pause the recording if you need to.
  Questions
  Have you been away?
  Did you have a good time?
  What's it like?
  Is there a lot to do?

EXERCISE

Match the subjects (1–12) with the questions (a–l).

1	Experience	a	How did you get there?
2	Frequency of travel	b	How far is it from ... (place) to ... (place)?
3	Place	c	How long does it take to fly to ... (place)?
4	Transport	d	Have you ever been to ... (place)?
5	Distance	e	Do you go there often?
6	Journey time	f	Where did you go exactly?
7	General comments	g	Did you have any problems?
8	Food	h	What did you do there?
9	Activities	i	What's the food like?
10	Sights	j	Is it a safe place?
11	Security	k	Is there much to see there?
12	Problems	l	How was it?

1 ▦ 2 ▦ 3 ▦ 4 ▦ 5 ▦ 6 ▦ 7 ▦ 8 ▦ 9 ▦ 10 ▦ 11 ▦ 12 ▦

Now listen and check your answers.

PRACTICE

Now listen again and practise asking the questions.

OVER TO YOU

**Play the questions again and answer each of the questions about the last
holiday you went on.**

4 Small talk questions about people and places

MODEL

1 Louis Danon and Marina Fusco are talking to each other over lunch at
  the same conference as in Listening unit 2. Listen to them talking and
  answer these questions.

How long has Marina been living in Paris?
Where does Louis live now?

2 **Now listen again and note down the questions Louis and Marina ask each other. Pause the recording if you need to.**

EXERCISE

Read the questions below. You will hear answers to eight of the questions. Write down the number of the questions in the order in which they are answered.

1	Origin	Where are you from originally?
2	Born	Where were you born?
3	Move to a place	When did you move to ... (place)?
4	Time in a place	How long have you lived / have you been living in ... (place)?
5	Population	What's the population of ... (place)?
6	Employment	Who's the main employer in the area?
7	Home	Where do you live?
8	Marriage	Are you married?
9	Children	Do you have any children?
10	Age of children	How old are they?
11	Partner's job	What does your partner do?
12	Hobbies and interests	What do you do in your spare time?

Now check your answers on page 84.

PRACTICE

Now listen and practise asking the questions.

OVER TO YOU

Play the questions again and answer each of the questions about people and places you know.

5 Presenting 1: Progress reports

MODEL

1 **Pam Henderson works in human resources. Listen to Pam presenting a progress report and answer these questions.**
What was the main objective of the project?
What was the secondary objective of the project?

2 **Now listen again. Pause the recording if you need to and note down the phrases Pam uses to:**
• **give the background to the current situation**
   To begin .... this project.
• **explain what has been done so far**
   I think we've .... progress.

• say what still has to be done or what will happen

.... speed up the training programme.

EXERCISE

Match the functions (1–3) with the sentences (a–f).

1 Giving the background to the current situation
2 Explaining what has been done so far
3 Saying what still has to be done or what will happen

a *We began this project in order to* improve profitability.
b *Then we plan to* run the same project in Portugal.
c *What we've done so far is* complete the first main stage.
d *The background to this project is* a drive to reduce costs.
e *We've already finished* the initial assessments.
f *The next stage is to* start the training programme.

1 ▓ ▓   2 ▓ ▓   3 ▓ ▓

Now listen and check your answers.

PRACTICE

Now listen again and practise saying the sentences.

OVER TO YOU

Imagine you are giving a presentation to a group of people about a project you're working on. Try to complete each of the phrases in the Exercise with your own ideas.

Listen to the phrases again and then practise saying your sentences.

6 Presenting 2: Structuring

MODEL

1 **Clive Williams is a health and safety officer. Listen to Clive introducing a new programme and answer these questions.**
What is the subject of his presentation?
What is the objective for next year?

2 **Now listen again. Pause the recording if you need to and note down the phrases Clive uses to:**
   • **clearly state the subject of the presentation at the beginning**
     Right, ... the new health and safety programme.
   • **say how long he will talk**
     I'll try to be brief ....
   • **signal a different part of the talk**
     Right, ... presentation, ...
   • **say the audience can ask questions**
     Are there .... ?

Match the functions (1–4) with the sentences (a–h).

1 Clearly stating the subject of the presentation at the beginning
2 Saying how long you will talk
3 Signalling the different parts of the talk
4 Saying the audience can ask questions

a *If you have any questions*, just interrupt me.
b *My talk is about* the reorganisation of the company.
c *I'm planning to talk for* around 30 minutes.
d *Firstly, I'll describe* the new system.
e *Finally, I'll present* the most important changes.
f *I'm going to talk about* the changes we're implementing.
g *My talk will last* about three quarters of an hour.
h *I'll answer questions* at the end.

1 ▦ ▦   2 ▦ ▦   3 ▦ ▦   4 ▦ ▦

Now listen and check your answers.

PRACTICE

Now listen again and practise saying the sentences.

OVER TO YOU

Imagine you are giving a presentation to a group of people at work. Try to complete each of the phrases in the Exercise with your own ideas.

Listen to the phrases again and then practise saying your sentences.

7 Presenting 3: Using visual supports

MODEL

1 **Clare Miller works for a museum. Listen to Clare giving a presentation about the museum and answer these questions.**
   How many different kinds of visual supports does Clare describe?
   What are they?

2 **Now listen again. Pause the recording if you need to and note down the phrases Clare uses to describe the visual supports.**
   • .... the layout of the museum and its exhibition spaces.
   • .... the layout is very simple.
   • .... changing visitor numbers at different times of the year.
   • ... in the summer months. ....

Match the sentences (1–6) with the pictures (a–f).

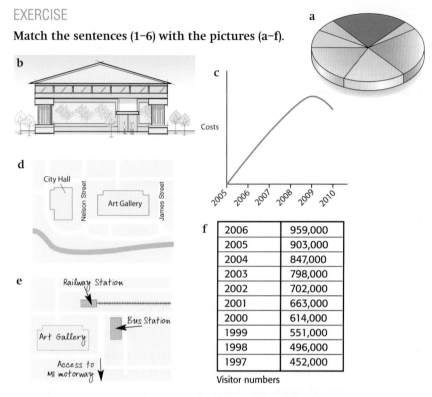

Costs

2005 2006 2007 2008 2009 2010

f		
	2006	959,000
	2005	903,000
	2004	847,000
	2003	798,000
	2002	702,000
	2001	663,000
	2000	614,000
	1999	551,000
	1998	496,000
	1997	452,000

Visitor numbers

1   *The first picture shows* the design for the outside of the new art gallery.
2   *This is a map showing* the location of the gallery, close to the waterfront and opposite the City Hall.
3   *You can see from the diagram I've drawn that* transport links are good as the bus and railway stations are both nearby.
4   Now *let's look at a pie chart showing* where the money is coming from to pay for the project.
5   Now *look at the table here showing* visitor numbers to the city over ten years.
6   Finally, *here is a graph* showing the projected costs over five years.

1 ▨   2 ▨   3 ▨   4 ▨   5 ▨   6 ▨

Now listen and check your answers.

PRACTICE

Now listen again and practise saying the sentences.

OVER TO YOU

Imagine you are giving a presentation to a group of people at work that requires you to use visual supports. Complete each of the phrases in the Exercise with your own ideas.

Listen to the phrases again and then practise saying your sentences.

8 Meetings 1: Listening and helping understanding

MODEL

1 Richard Dean works in research and development. Listen to Richard chairing a meeting with Anna and Fritz and answer these questions.
   What are the participants talking about?
   What problem do they have?

2 Now listen again. Pause the recording if you need to and note down the ways Richard, Anna and Fritz show they are listening and helping each other to understand.

EXERCISE

Match the functions (1–5) with the sentences (a–j).

1 Paraphrasing
2 Asking for repetition
3 Checking that people understand you
4 Showing you understand
5 Showing you're interested and are listening

a It's all rather complicated. *Shall I go through it again?*
b Yes, *that's very clear.*
c *Do you mean that* Alex is now going to be leading the project?
d *Could you repeat* what you said earlier?
e *I see what you mean.*
f So, *in other words* we're delaying the release date?
g *Can you say that again?*
h *Do you want me to* give another example?
i *Really?*
j *That's interesting.*

   1 ▧ ▧ 2 ▧ ▧ 3 ▧ ▧ 4 ▧ ▧ 5 ▧ ▧

Now listen and check your answers.

PRACTICE

Now listen again and practise saying the sentences.

OVER TO YOU

Listen to six sentences from different meetings. For each one, respond appropriately to show you are listening actively. Try to use as many of the strategies in the Exercise as you can.

9 Meetings 2: Teleconferencing

MODEL

1 Sara Cliff has set up a teleconference with some colleagues in different locations. Listen to the teleconference and answer these questions.

How many people do you hear taking part in the teleconference?
What are they trying to organise?

2 **Now listen again. Pause the recording if you need to and note down the phrases Sara uses to:**
- **check everyone can hear**
  Right, ...
- **set out the rules of the teleconference**
  OK, please speak ....
  If you don't ....
  And, please, just one ....
- **ask a participant to repeat something**
  I missed that. Can .... ?

EXERCISE

Match the functions (1–4) with the sentences (a–h).
1 Giving teleconference rules
2 Saying you have technical problems
3 Saying you have language problems
4 Checking understanding

a I'm sorry, *I can't hear you very well.*
b Can you say that in different words? *I can't understand everything you're saying.*
c *Please try not to talk at the same time.* It's difficult to follow what is being said.
d Sorry, *I don't know what that means.* Can you explain?
e *It's very important to speak slowly and clearly.*
f *I'd like to check I understand what you said. Can I read it back to you?*
g *Did you say* you want the report next week?
h Unfortunately, *the line's really bad and I can't hear anything.*

1 ▓ ▓   2 ▓ ▓   3 ▓ ▓   4 ▓ ▓

Now listen and check your answers.

PRACTICE

Now listen again and practise saying the sentences.

OVER TO YOU

Imagine you are taking part in a teleconference. You will hear six people saying different things. Respond to each sentence appropriately.

10 Meetings 3: Summarising and closing

MODEL

1 **Tom Harvey has been chairing a meeting with colleagues. Listen to Tom summarising and closing the meeting and answer these questions.**

What is the main conclusion of the meeting?
What will Tom do on Monday?

2 **Now listen again. Pause the recording if you need to and note down the phrases Tom uses to:**
   • **praise the quality of the meeting**
     OK, well ....
   • **say that time is running out**
     It's almost ....
   • **summarise what has been agreed**
     I'd like to .... of the meeting.
   • **state the main action point**
     I'll .... how much is available.
   • **ask if there is anything else important to say before closing**
     Now, ... ?
   • **close the meeting**
     So, ... everyone.

EXERCISE

Match the functions (1–6) with the sentences (a–f).
1 Praising the quality of the meeting
2 Saying that time is running out
3 Summarising what has been agreed
4 Stating the main action point
5 Asking if there is anything else important to say before closing
6 Closing the meeting

a *Marie will commission a report on this by the end of March.*
b *Does anyone have any final comments?*
c *Time's almost up – we only have this room until two.*
d *We're all in agreement that we need to ask for more time on this.*
e *That's all, then. Thank you to everyone for coming.* See you next week.
f *It's been a productive meeting.*

1 ▦ 2 ▦ 3 ▦ 4 ▦ 5 ▦ 6 ▦

Now listen and check your answers.

PRACTICE

Now listen again and practise saying the sentences.

OVER TO YOU

Think of a meeting you attended recently. What was the main outcome of the meeting?

Imagine you are in the meeting again and are chairing it. You only have a few minutes left. Summarise and close the meeting for the group, using the phrases in the Exercise to help you.

11 Negotiating 1: Stating positive expectations and preferences, suggesting alternatives

MODEL

1 Vicky Palmer is an architect. She is working on the design for a new office building for Mark Davidson's company. Listen to Vicky and Mark negotiating and answer these questions.
How has Vicky changed the design of the reception area?
What three features do they discuss for the reception area?

2 Now listen again. Pause the recording if you need to and note down the phrases Vicky and Mark use to:
  • state positive expectations
  I think ....
  Yes, I'm looking ....
  • state preferences
  I'd .... on one side ...
  I'd .... that.
  • suggest alternatives.
  But what .... in the middle ...?
  Another .... some ...

EXERCISE

Listen to six sentences (a–f) and match them with the functions (1–3). For each one, write 1, 2 or 3 below.
1 Stating positive expectations
2 Stating preferences
3 Suggesting alternatives

  a ▨ b ▨ c ▨ d ▨ e ▨ f ▨

Now check your answers on page 87.

PRACTICE

Now listen and practise saying the sentences.

OVER TO YOU

Think of a situation at work or at home in which you will have to negotiate soon. Note down some ways in which you will state positive expectations at the beginning of the negotiation and any preferences you have. Finally, think about what you will say if your preferences are not fully accepted and write down some alternative suggestions.

Now practise saying your sentences.

12 Negotiating 2: Bargaining and reaching a compromise

MODEL

1 Kate Spellman is making arrangements for a company conference.

Andrew Holt represents the conference venue where Kate's company is going to hold the conference. Listen to Kate and Andrew bargaining and reaching a compromise, and answer these questions.

What does Kate want from the negotiation?
What does Andrew want?
What compromise do they reach?

2 Now listen again. Pause the recording if you need to and note down the phrases Kate and Andrew use to:
- **ask for a discount**
  What .... ?
- **politely refuse**
  Unfortunately, ... any more.
  No, I .... that.
- **suggest a compromise**
  But I can .... if you pay ...
  Well, we'd .... stages.
- **agree to a compromise**
  OK, that's fine. We'll .... – you're old clients ...
  That's .... So, ...
  Agreed.

EXERCISE

The sentences are taken from a negotiation but they are in the wrong order. Put the sentences in the correct order to complete the conversation. The first one is done for you.

▦ Good. So it's €85 per unit, with you paying for transport and insurance.

▦ What do you say to €80 as we'll be paying for the transport and insurance anyway?

▦ Agreed.

▦ I don't think we can accept that. It's too low. How about €85?

▦ I'm not sure about that. You see, we normally take care of the transport and insurance – we do that ourselves anyway.

▦ That sounds reasonable. I'm sure we can agree to that.

1 If we agree a price of €100 per unit, can you agree to pay all the transportation and insurance costs?

▦ OK, well, I think in that case we can reduce the price to €90.

Now listen and check your answers.

PRACTICE

Now listen again and practise saying the sentences.

OVER TO YOU

Imagine you are in a negotiation. You will hear the person you are negotiating with saying six different things. Respond to each sentence appropriately.

Part 2 Pronunciation

In this part, you can listen again and practise the pronunciation work in the type 1 units in the *English365* Student's Book 3 and practise repeating key phrases.

1 Minimal pairs (see Student's Book Unit 1)

Each nationality has different problems pronouncing sounds in English. Listen to the pronunciation of these minimal pairs and the example sentences and then repeat them.

1 live / leave
  I live in the city centre. / I leave the office every day at seven o'clock.
2 would / word
  I would like to visit Martinique. / It's a difficult word to pronounce.
3 plane / plan
  My plane is at seven. / My plan is to leave at seven.
4 sheet / cheat
  I need a sheet of paper. / I never cheat when I play cards!
5 wet / vet
  It's very wet today. / I need to take my cat to the vet.
6 thought / sort
  I thought the documents were interesting. / I sort my documents every weekend.
7 ban / van
  I think a better solution is a ban. / I think a better solution is a van.
8 price / prize
  The price was very good. / The prize was very good.
9 wall / war
  The wall was difficult to build. / The war was difficult to stop.
10 length / lens
  We need to check the length. / We need to check the lens.

2 Using pauses to add impact (see Student's Book Unit 4)

We can add impact to the way we speak by using pauses after the connecting words which build our message. In addition, we can pronounce the connecting words with extra stress to focus the listener's attention. Listen to the way the speaker adds impact to the message and repeat each sentence.

This product has three main benefits. *Firstly*, it's more reliable than anything else on the market. *In addition*, we support it with excellent after-sales service. *As a result*, you have total peace of mind. And *finally*, the price is very, very competitive. *In fact*, we believe we have the best cost-benefit package on the market.

3 Emphasising important words (see Student's Book Unit 7)

We emphasise different words in the same sentence depending on the situation. Listen to the different emphasis in these sentences and repeat each sentence.

1 Did you say <u>you</u> would post the report to me?
   Did you say you would <u>post</u> the report to me?
2 I'm not free on Monday <u>morning</u>.
   I'm not free on <u>Monday</u> morning.
3 I <u>think</u> it's my suitcase.
   I think it's <u>my</u> suitcase.
4 Could I <u>observe</u> the team-building seminar?
   Could <u>I</u> observe the team-building seminar?
5 <u>I</u> didn't delete all of this data.
   I didn't delete <u>all</u> of this data.

4 Polite disagreement in short answers (see Student's Book Unit 10)

Many native speakers of English express polite disagreement in short answers by speaking with a little hesitation, stressing key words such as *could*, *may* or *possible* and speaking with a higher and/or slightly weaker tone of voice. Listen and repeat the short answers.

1 A: I think that increasing computer memory will solve the software problem.
   B: Yes, it seems so.
2 A: I think the answer is to reinstall the software.
   B: Yes, I think so.
3 A: I think this new IT system could save us a lot of money.
   B: It's possible, yes.
4 A: I think outsourcing is cheaper.
   B: You might be right.
5 A: It looks as if we're going to finish the project on time.
   B: Yes, you could be right.

5 Stress in word families (see Student's Book Unit 13)

When we build families of words (nouns, verbs, adjectives, etc.), the syllable that is stressed can change. Listen and repeat each word in these word families.

1 competition	competitive	competitor	compete
2 analysis	analytical	analyst	analyse
3 negotiation	negotiable	negotiator	negotiate
4 organisation	organised	organiser	organise
5 management	managerial	manager	manage
6 innovation	innovative	innovator	innovate

6 Adding impact and interest (see Student's Book Unit 16)

We can make our message more interesting by using adverbs to give impact to what we say. We also use pronunciation to add impact by increasing the range of our pitch and tone, increasing volume and stress and pausing for effect. Listen to the conversation and repeat speaker B's sentences.

A: How was your trip to Shanghai?
B: Great. Unfortunately, it was only a few days.
A: Did you enjoy it?
B: Yes, people in China are always amazingly friendly. I'd go back immediately if I had the chance.

7 Linking (see Student's Book Unit 19)

Native speakers link words together in a number of different ways when speaking quickly. Listen and repeat these sentences.

1 I usually read the newspaper first thing in the morning.
2 I read an interesting article about creativity today.
3 My internet provider publishes regular news updates.
4 One television programme which I like is *Newsnight* on BBC2.
5 I read two or three magazines a month.
6 Several British newspapers are owned by Rupert Murdoch.

8 Modal verbs with *have* in third conditional sentences
(see Student's Book Unit 22)

In the non-*if* clause, *have* is pronounced with a schwa as /əv/ and links to the modal verb before it. For example, *would have* is pronounced /wʊdəv/, *wouldn't have* /wʊntəv/, *could have* /kʊdəv/, *couldn't have* /kʊntəv/ and *might have* /maɪtəv/. When we contract *would*, the pronoun is pronounced with /dəv/ following it. For example, *I'd have* /aɪdəv/, *you'd have* /juːdəv/, etc. Listen and repeat these sentences.

1 If you'd told me about the problem, I'd have helped.
2 She'd have come to the meeting if she'd had time.
3 If I hadn't gone to the interview, I couldn't have got the job.
4 They might have got it by now if you'd sent the package a day earlier.
5 If you'd saved the file first, you wouldn't have lost it.
6 If we'd reached our targets, we'd have got a very good bonus.

9 Chunking and pausing (see Student's Book Unit 25)

When speaking we normally 'chunk' words together and use pauses around these chunks. In written English we can see many of these pauses as commas and full stops. We usually pause in logical places, after clauses or word groups, e.g. *at the moment*. Listen to the chunking and pauses in this recording of Nelson Mandela's words, and then repeat the sentences.

Friends / comrades / and fellow South Africans. / I greet you all / in the name of peace / democracy / and freedom for all. / I stand here before you / not as a prophet / but as a humble servant / of you / the people. / On this day of my release / I extend my warmest gratitude / to the millions of my compatriots / and those in every corner of the globe / who have campaigned tirelessly / for my release.

10 Spelling and pronunciation (see Student's Book Unit 28)

English spelling causes difficulties for many students because the same letters can have totally different sounds. In each group below one word has a different pronunciation from the other three words. Listen and repeat each word.

1	'h'	honest	hour	hope	honour
2	'wh'	what	while	whole	which
3	'ng'	finger	singer	hunger	anger
4	'l'	talk	salmon	half	film
5	'ea'	health	heard	leather	death
6	'u'	rude	conclusion	pudding	flute
7	's'	please	choose	increase	lose
8	'a'	danger	grateful	trade	all
9	'g'	strength	resign	foreigner	signature
10	'th'	thin	through	then	think

Tapescript: Part 1 Models

1 Small talk questions about work

JULIE: So, Ken, what do you do exactly? I know you work in Birmingham.

KEN: Yes, I'm Head of Customer Services there.

JULIE: How long have you worked for ICF?

KEN: Quite a long time now. I suppose it must be around eight years.

JULIE: And how long have you been in customer services?

KEN: About two years now. Before that I worked in sales.

JULIE: I was in sales for a long time too. Are you looking forward to working on this project?

KEN: Yes, it sounds very interesting.

JULIE: What's your role on the project?

KEN: My brief is to go out and meet people, do the initial data gathering and get to know how the different North American organisations handle customer services.

JULIE: Yes, it sounds an interesting role. So when did you join the project team? I know you weren't at the kick-off meeting.

KEN: No, I arrived just last week. That's why we haven't really met yet.

JULIE: Well, I'm sure we'll be seeing a lot of each other in the future.

KEN: And what about you, Julie? How ...

2 Small talk questions about organisations and business

LOUIS: So, who do you work for?

MARINA: I work for Modella.

LOUIS: Modella. Is that a fashion company? What does it do?

MARINA: Yes, it's part of the Italian Alta Group.

LOUIS: I know. We did some work for Alta last year. So, what are your main products in France?

MARINA: Well, we specialise in sports fashion, mainly swimming, surfing, diving ...

LOUIS: I see. And how's business at the moment? It's been a good summer.

MARINA: Oh, it's not so easy. Sales are down a little. The competition's very tough.

LOUIS: I can imagine. Who's your main competitor?

MARINA: There are a lot, unfortunately. I guess Surftech is one of the biggest. It's huge.

LOUIS: Really? So how many people work for Modella?

MARINA: We're quite small, about five hundred at the moment altogether. And in France there are just over one hundred. But after the next reorganisation this may decrease, I suppose.

LOUIS: Yes, we're restructuring at the moment too.

MARINA: Oh, I hope it's not too difficult ...

3 Small talk questions about holidays

JULIE: Ian, good to see you.

IAN: Good to see you too. Peter told me you would be here.

JULIE: Yes, just for the week. You look very well. Have you been away?

IAN: Yes, we got back from South Africa last night.

JULIE: South Africa! Fantastic! Did you have a good time?

IAN: We had a great time.

JULIE: Good. So what's it like?

IAN: It's amazing. Beaches, sunshine ... I feel really relaxed now.

JULIE: Is there a lot to do?

IAN: Walking, diving, sunbathing ... you name it.

JULIE: I can't imagine you diving or doing much walking.

IAN: That's true. You know me too well. Jane went walking – I just sat on the beach all day.

JULIE: Well, it obviously did you good! We're going to Slovenia at the end of June.

IAN: Really? There was a programme about Slovenia on ...

4 Small talk questions about people and places

LOUIS: So where are you from originally, Marina?

MARINA: I'm from Rome actually, and all my family are there, but I haven't been back for a few months.

LOUIS: And so how long have you been living in Paris?

MARINA: Since January last year. It didn't take me long to make up my mind when I got the offer of the job.

LOUIS: Did you want to live abroad?

MARINA: Oh, yes, and I've always liked France.

LOUIS: Have you found somewhere nice to live in Paris?

MARINA: Yeah, I've got a very nice flat – quite central, with everything I need nearby.

LOUIS: Sounds good.

MARINA: It is. And how about you? Where do you live? Are you from Paris?

LOUIS: No, I was born in Grenoble, and now we live in the country near Lyon.

MARINA: Oh, yes, I've been to Lyon. Do you like living in the country?

LOUIS: Yes, I'm really glad we're not in a city any more, and the children seem very happy.

MARINA: Do you go for lots of long walks?

LOUIS: No, not really. With three young children I don't have much spare time.

MARINA: How old are they?

LOUIS: The oldest ...

5 Presenting 1: Progress reports

PAM: To begin, I'd just like to restate the main objective of this project. As I'm sure you'll all remember, we began last year with the objective of reducing costs by 15%. OK, it was a tough target, but I think we've made very good progress. We've already cut the number of personnel from forty-five to thirty-five through a mix of relocation and early retirement. We had expected this to be a little painful but, in fact, this phase of the project has gone very, very smoothly. So, we're certainly on target to reach the thirty we need by the end of the year. As regards the secondary objective, completing the training on the new system, unfortunately, only a third of relevant staff have completed the in-house training we set up. So there are a lot of people who haven't begun yet. And this is what we need to discuss and plan today. The next stage is to decide how to speed up the training programme. So, if there are no questions on that, we can perhaps begin the meeting.

6 Presenting 2: Structuring

CLIVE: OK, shall we get started? Right, I'm here to talk about the new health and safety programme. My main objective is really just to give you more information about the schedule as the programme starts next month. I'll try to be brief so that we can be finished by 11 o'clock. I hope that's OK. To begin, by way of background I'd like to spend a few minutes looking at the current health and safety system and its problems. Then I'll outline the new rules and I'll spend some time looking at fire regulations. Then – and this is the real objective – I'll outline the schedule.

* * * * *

Right, I'd like to move on to the second part of the presentation, the new rules on fire safety. Now, I know this is going to repeat some of the points I've already discussed about reporting processes but I think it's useful to repeat key points sometimes.

* * * * *

Finally, before I finish, I just want to repeat the key message again. The objective for next year is to have a 100% – that's a 100% – injury-free year here. This means not only knowing the new safety rules but also and more importantly, making sure that everyone follows them. So, that's really all I wanted to say. Are there any questions about anything I've said today?

7 Presenting 3: Using visual supports

CLARE: So first of all this is the structure of my talk. First, some general comments about the museum. Then a closer look at the key characteristics of the museum. And finally, a few words about future plans.
Here is a diagram of the layout of the museum and its exhibition spaces. You can see that the layout is very simple.
And here we have a graph showing changing visitor numbers at different times of the year. Obviously, there are more visitors in the summer months. That's very clear from the graph.

8 Meetings 1: Listening and helping understanding

RICHARD: OK, next on the agenda is the Poland trip.
ANNA: Yes. When are we going to find out about the research trip there?
RICHARD: Well, it's possible that we're going to have our travel budgets cut.
FRITZ: Cut our travel budgets? Does this mean the trip is cancelled?
RICHARD: Not necessarily, but I think it's going to be difficult to do everything we planned.
ANNA: Do you mean we'll be sending fewer people?
RICHARD: Probably, but we can wait and see.
FRITZ: I see. When will we know how many we can send? This could affect what we'll be able to do over there.
RICHARD: We should know next week. When we find out, we can look at our objectives again and match them against the resources we have.
ANNA: So, in other words we might have to make cuts?
RICHARD: That might happen but we'll wait and see.
FRITZ: OK, we understand. Let's talk about this again next week when we know more.

9 Meetings 2: Teleconferencing

SARA: Right, can you all hear me all right?
KARL/ICHIRO/LUISA: Yes. It's fine. Very clear.
SARA: Right. OK, please speak slowly and clearly. If you don't understand something, please ask someone to repeat it. And, please, just one person should speak at any one time. Now, we need to talk about the meeting next month in London – we have to organise this meeting this week. I think everyone is coming, right?
KARL: No, unfortunately I can't come. We've got a big conference in Budapest and I have to go to that.
SARA: Sorry, Karl, I missed that. Can you say that again?
KARL: There's a conference in Budapest that we're organising so I have to go to that.
SARA: You can't come? OK, that's a pity, but I understand.
ICHIRO: Maybe we should change the date?
LUISA: No, I don't think so … it's too late to change the date.
SARA: Yes, you're right. I think we agree we can't change the date at this point. It's too late.

10 Meetings 3: Summarising and closing

TOM: OK, well it's been a really useful meeting. It's almost four and time to finish. I'd like to summarise the main recommendation from the meeting. I think we all agree that we need to spend more time and more money on market research for this project. Things have already changed a lot in a very short time from when we first discussed this. The market has changed a lot – Karen has made this very clear in her report. This means we have to try and find more budget for market research and I'll talk to Mike next week about how much is available. Now, is there anything else? I'll send an email out about this on Monday and if anyone wants to talk about it further, just call me. So, I think that's all for now. Thanks to everyone.

11 Negotiating 1: Stating positive expectations and preferences, suggesting alternatives

VICKY: After our last meeting, I know you wanted to change a few things in the design, so I've done some new drawings for you to look at and I think you'll like them.

MARK: Yes, I'm looking forward to seeing the new ideas.

VICKY: Have a look. You'll see I've changed the size of the reception area as you wanted. It's now much bigger and it's also much lighter because of the big windows here.

MARK: Oh, yes, that's good. I wonder whether you could move the door to a different position. I'd prefer the main door to be on one side rather than in the middle.

VICKY: Well, we could do that, but what about keeping it in the middle and making a special feature of it? We could make the main door look interesting. Another possibility is to have some big plants you see as soon as you walk through the door.

MARK: I like the idea of making it look attractive, but I don't think we want too many plants, do you? I'd rather not do that.

VICKY: No, you're probably right. Well, why not have a beautiful sculpture rather than plants? I've got some ideas I can show you.

MARK: Yes, that might be very good. Let's look at your suggestions.

12 Negotiating 2: Bargaining and reaching a compromise

KATE: So, we need to discuss the price. What about a good discount for us?

ANDREW: Unfortunately, we don't think we can lower the price any more. The price is very competitive, and only a little more expensive than last year.

KATE: Yes, but this year we have more people coming so it will cost us a lot more. Anyway, I'm sure you could manage a small discount – let's say ten per cent?

ANDREW: No, I don't think I can do that. And I'd like to have the payment earlier. But I can offer a four per cent reduction if you pay the total amount 60 days before the conference date.

KATE: Well, first of all, everyone knows that the mid-point between zero and ten is five.

ANDREW: OK, five per cent it is, but with the payment 60 days beforehand.

KATE: Well, we'd prefer to pay in two stages. How about 50 per cent 60 days before, and 50 per cent a week before the conference?

ANDREW: OK, that's fine. We'll say yes to that – you're old clients of ours, so we'll agree.

KATE: That's good, thank you. So, a five per cent reduction, with payment in two stages.

ANDREW: Agreed.

Answer key to Listening units

1 Small talk questions about work
Model
1 He is Head of Customer Services in Birmingham.
  He joined the project team last week.
2 What do you do exactly?
  How long have you worked for …?
  How long have you been in …?
  Are you looking forward to working on this project?
  What's your role on the project?
  When did you join the project team?
Exercise
3, 1, 5, 2, 8, 10, 12, 11

2 Small talk questions about organisations and business
Model
1 She works for a fashion company.
  About five hundred people work at the company altogether
  at the moment.
2 Who do you work for?
  Is that a fashion company? What does it do?
  What are your main products in …?
  How's business at the moment?
  Who's your main competitor?
  How many people work for …?
Exercise
8, 4, 11, 1, 6, 3, 7, 9

3 Small talk questions about holidays
Model
1 He went to South Africa.
  He sat on the beach all day.
2 Yes, we got back from South Africa last night.
  We had a great time.
  It's amazing.
  Walking, diving, sunbathing …
Exercise
1 d   2 e   3 f   4 a   5 b   6 c   7 l
8 i   9 h   10 k   11 j   12 g

4 Small talk questions about people and places
Model
1 She's been living in Paris since January last year.
  He lives in the country near Lyon.

2 Louis
   Where are you from originally?
   How long have you been living in ...?
   Did you want to live abroad?
   Have you found somewhere nice to live in ...?
   Marina
   And how about you?
   Where do you live?
   Are you from ...?
   Do you like living in the country?
   Do you go for lots of long walks?
   How old are they?
Exercise
5, 11, 1, 4, 2, 6, 9, 12

5 Presenting 1: Progress reports
Model
1 The main objective was to reduce costs by 15%.
   The secondary objective was completing the training on the
   new system.
2 To begin, I'd just like to restate the main objective of this project.
   I think we've made very good progress.
   The next stage is to decide how to speed up the training programme.
Exercise
1 a, d   2 c, e   3 b, f

6 Presenting 2: Structuring
Model
1 The subject of his presentation is the new health and safety
   programme.
   The objective for next year is to have a 100% injury-free year.
2 Right, I'm here to talk about the new health and safety programme.
   I'll try to be brief so that we can be finished by 11 o'clock.
   Right, I'd like to move on to the second part of the presentation, ...
   Are there any questions about anything I've said today?
Exercise
1 b, f   2 c, g   3 d, e   4 a, h

7 Presenting 3: Using visual supports
Model
1 She describes two visual supports: a diagram and a graph.
2 Here is a diagram of the layout of the museum and its exhibition spaces.
   You can see that the layout is very simple.
   And here we have a graph showing changing visitor numbers at different
   times of the year.
   ... in the summer months. That's very clear from the graph.
Exercise
1 b   2 d   3 e   4 a   5 f   6 c

8 Meetings 1: Listening and helping understanding

Model

1 They are talking about a research trip to Poland.
  They may not be able to do all they had planned because of possible cuts to the budget.
2 They show they are actively listening by saying things like 'Yes', 'I see', 'OK, we understand'.
  They paraphrase in order to check their understanding, for example, 'So, in other words we might have to make cuts?'
  They also repeat what the speaker before them has said, for example, 'Cut our travel budgets?'

Exercise

1 c, f   2 d, g   3 a, h   4 b, e   5 i, j

9 Meetings 2: Teleconferencing

Model

1 Four people are taking part in the teleconference.
  They are trying to organise a meeting next month in London.
2 Right, can you all hear me all right?
  OK, please speak slowly and clearly.
  If you don't understand something, please ask someone to repeat it.
  And, please, just one person should speak at any one time.
  I missed that. Can you say that again?

Exercise

1 c, e   2 a, h   3 b, d   4 f, g

10 Meetings 3: Summarising and closing

Model

1 They need to spend more time and money on market research.
  He will send an email about it on Monday.
2 OK, well it's been a really useful meeting.
  It's almost four and time to finish.
  I'd like to summarise the main recommendation from the meeting.
  I'll talk to Mike next week about how much is available.
  Now, is there anything else?
  So, I think that's all for now. Thanks to everyone.

Exercise

1 f   2 c   3 d   4 a   5 b   6 e

11 Negotiating 1: Stating positive expectations and preferences, suggesting alternatives

Model

1 The reception area is much bigger and lighter.
They discuss the door, plants and a sculpture.
2 I think you'll like them.
Yes, I'm looking forward to seeing the new ideas.
I'd prefer the main door to be on one side ...
I'd rather not do that.
But what about keeping it in the middle ...?
Another possibility is to have some ...

Exercise

a 3 b 2 c 1 d 2 e 3 f 1

12 Negotiating 2: Bargaining and reaching a compromise

Model

1 Kate wants a good discount on the price.
Andrew wants the payment earlier.
The compromise is a five per cent reduction with payment in two stages.
2 What about a good discount for us?
Unfortunately, we don't think we can lower the price any more.
No, I don't think I can do that.
But I can offer a four per cent reduction if you pay ...
Well, we'd prefer to pay in two stages.
OK, that's fine. We'll say yes to that – you're old clients ...
That's good, thank you. So, ...
Agreed.

Exercise

1 If we agree a price of €100 per unit, can you agree to pay all the transportation and insurance costs?
2 I'm not sure about that. You see, we normally take care of the transport and insurance – we do that ourselves anyway.
3 OK, well, I think in that case we can reduce the price to €90.
4 What do you say to €80 as we'll be paying for the transport and insurance anyway?
5 I don't think we can accept that. It's too low. How about €85?
6 That sounds reasonable. I'm sure we can agree to that.
7 Good. So it's €85 per unit, with you paying for transport and insurance.
8 Agreed.

Learning diaries

Learning diary 1: Grammar

Progress	Which areas of my grammar have improved?

Classroom learning	Which learning activities in the classroom helped me learn grammar?

Self-study	What have I done outside the classroom to practise or improve my grammar?

Problems	Which grammar mistakes do I still find it difficult to correct?

Priorities	Which grammar areas should I focus on now?

Future learning action plan

Every time you write in your grammar diary, note down any other experiences, thoughts or feelings about developing your grammar, particularly any *new ideas* you have for learning, which can help you create an action plan to improve more quickly in the future.

English365 Personal Study Book 3 © Cambridge University Press 2005

Learning diary 2: Communications skills

Answer the questions for communication skills.

Progress	Which areas of my communication skills have I improved?
Classroom learning	Which learning activities in the classroom helped me to improve?
Self-study	What have I done outside the classroom to practise or improve my communication skills?
Problems	What do I still need to improve?
Priorities	Which areas of my communication skills should I focus on now?

Telephoning

Presenting

Meetings

Negotiations

Emails

Social skills

Future learning action plan
Every time you write in your communication skills diary, note down any other experiences, thoughts or feelings about developing your communication skills, particularly any *new ideas* you have for learning, which can help you create an action plan to improve more quickly in the future.

English365 Personal Study Book 3 © Cambridge University Press 2005

Learning diary 3: Vocabulary

Answer the questions for both business and general vocabulary.

Progress   Which areas of vocabulary have I improved?

Classroom learning Which learning activities in the classroom helped
                      me to improve?

Self-study   What have I done outside the classroom to practise
                      or increase my vocabulary?

Problems   What do I still need to improve?

Priorities   Which areas of my vocabulary should I focus on now?

Business vocabulary

General vocabulary

Future learning action plan
Every time you write in your vocabulary diary, note down any other
experiences, thoughts or feelings about developing your vocabulary,
particularly any *new ideas* you have for learning, which can help you create
an action plan to improve more quickly in the future.

English365 Personal Study Book 3 © Cambridge University Press 2005

Learning diary 4: Speaking fluently

Progress   How much has my fluency improved?

Classroom learning   Which learning activities in the classroom helped
                      me to improve?

Self-study   What have I done outside the classroom to practise
                      or improve my fluency?

Problems   What is stopping me from becoming more fluent?

Priorities   In which situations do I need to focus on becoming
                      more fluent?

Future learning action plan

Every time you write in your speaking fluently diary, note down any other
experiences, thoughts or feelings about developing your fluency,
particularly any *new ideas* you have for learning, which can help you create
an action plan to improve more quickly in the future.

Learning diary 5: Pronunciation

Progress | How has my pronunciation improved?

Classroom learning | Which learning activities in the classroom helped me to improve?

Self-study | What have I done outside the classroom to practise or improve my pronunciation?

Problems | What do I still need to improve?

Priorities | Which areas of my pronunciation should I focus on now?

Future learning action plan

Every time you write in your pronunciation diary, note down any other experiences, thoughts or feelings about developing your pronunciation, particularly any *new ideas* you have for learning, which can help you create an action plan to improve more quickly in the future.

Learning diary 6: Understanding (listening and reading)

Answer the questions for both listening and reading.

Progress	How far has my understanding of English improved?
Classroom learning	Which learning activities in the classroom helped me to improve?
Self-study	What have I done outside the classroom to practise or improve my understanding?
Problems	What do I still need to improve?
Priorities	Which areas of my understanding should I focus on now?

Listening

Reading

Future learning action plan
Every time you write in your understanding diary, note down any other experiences, thoughts or feelings about developing listening and reading comprehension, particularly any *new ideas* you have for learning, which can help you create an action plan to improve more quickly in the future.

Track numbers

Track	Title	Time
1	Introduction	2:15
Part 1 Listening units		
	1 Small talk questions about work	
2	*Model*	1:47
3	*Exercise*	1:12
4	*Practice*	2:14
5	*Over to you*	0:09
	2 Small talk questions about organisations and business	
6	*Model*	1:54
7	*Exercise*	1:13
8	*Practice*	2:10
9	*Over to you*	0:11
	3 Small talk questions about holidays	
10	*Model*	1:34
11	*Exercise*	1:57
12	*Practice*	0:08
13	*Over to you*	0:10
	4 Small talk questions about people and places	
14	*Model*	1:53
15	*Exercise*	0:57
16	*Practice*	1:48
17	*Over to you*	0:11
	5 Presenting 1: Progress reports	
18	*Model*	2:07
19	*Exercise*	1:11
20	*Practice*	0:08
21	*Over to you*	0:23
	6 Presenting 2: Structuring	
22	*Model*	2:18
23	*Exercise*	1:26
24	*Practice*	0:08
25	*Over to you*	0:20
	7 Presenting 3: Using visual supports	
26	*Model*	1:21
27	*Exercise*	1:09
28	*Practice*	0:08
29	*Over to you*	0:23
	8 Meetings 1: Listening and helping understanding	
30	*Model*	1:40
31	*Exercise*	1:22
32	*Practice*	0:08
33	*Over to you*	1:12

9 Meetings 2: Teleconferencing
34	*Model*	1:55
35	*Exercise*	1:25
36	*Practice*	0:07
37	*Over to you*	1:18

10 Meetings 3: Summarising and closing
38	*Model*	1:59
39	*Exercise*	1:25
40	*Practice*	0:08
41	*Over to you*	0:25

11 Negotiating 1: Stating positive expectations and preferences, suggesting alternatives
42	*Model*	2:13
43	*Exercise*	1:16
44	*Practice*	0:55
45	*Over to you*	0:34

12 Negotiating 2: Bargaining and reaching a compromise
46	*Model*	2:26
47	*Exercise*	1:16
48	*Practice*	0:08
49	*Over to you*	1:00

Part 2 Pronunciation
50	1 Minimal pairs	2:56
51	2 Using pauses to add impact	1:04
52	3 Emphasising important words	1:06
53	4 Polite disagreement in short answers	1:15
54	5 Stress in word families	1:37
55	6 Adding impact and interest	0:51
56	7 Linking	1:30
57	8 Modal verbs with *have* in third conditional sentences	1:48
58	9 Chunking and pausing	1:23
59	10 Spelling and pronunciation	2:31

Thanks and acknowledgements

The authors would like to thank:

- Will Capel and Sally Searby of Cambridge University Press for their unflinching support from start to finish;
- Alison Silver for her eagle eye for detail, for her good sense and good cheer throughout the editorial and proofreading process;
- Matt Smelt-Webb for his helpful suggestions;
- Julie Moore for her help with the Do it yourself exercises, based on research from the Cambridge Learner Corpus;
- Helena Sharman for writing the worksheets for the Website;
- Sarah Hall for proofreading the Student's Book and Ruth Carim for proofreading the Teacher's Book and Personal Study Book;
- James Richardson for producing the recordings at Studio AVP, London;
- Sue Nicholas for the picture research;
- Hart McLeod for the design and page make-up;
- Sue Evans; Lorenza, Mathieu, Jérôme and Michael Flinders; and Lyn, Jude, Ruth and Neil Sweeney for their continuing patience;
- colleagues and friends at York Associates and in the School of Management, Community and Communication at York St John College for their tolerance of authorial distraction;
- and Chris Capper of Cambridge University Press for his immeasurable contribution to the project. It is above all his huge efforts which have made this book possible.

The authors and publishers are grateful to the following for permission to use copyright material. While every effort has been made, it has not been possible to identify the sources of all the material used and in such cases the publishers would welcome information from the copyright owners:
pp.14–18 word definitions extracted from *Cambridge Advanced Learner's Dictionary* (2003), edited by Patrick Gillard, published by Cambridge University Press.

The authors and publishers would like to thank the following for permission to reproduce photographs:
p.19 top ©Travel-Shots/Alamy, bottom ©Image100/Alamy; p.20 ©Gareth Bowden; p.23 ©Phil Schermeister/Corbis; p.27 ©Don Smith/Alamy; p.28 ©Yuriko Nakao/Reuters/Corbis; p.32 ©Corbis; p.33 ©Corbis; p.34 ©Jose Fuste Raga/Corbis; p.36 ©Travelstock44/Alamy; p.37 ©Snap/Rex Features; p.39 with kind permission of Random House; p.41 ©Lester Lefkowitz/Corbis.

Illustrations by Rupert Besley page 47; Tim Oliver page 70